W9-AWM-773

Oracle Applications DBA Field Guide

Elke Phelps
Paul Jackson

Apress®

Oracle Applications DBA Field Guide

Copyright © 2006 by Elke Phelps and Paul Jackson

All rights reserved. No part of this work may be reproduced or transmitted in any form or by any means, electronic or mechanical, including photocopying, recording, or by any information storage or retrieval system, without the prior written permission of the copyright owner and the publisher.

ISBN-13 (pbk): 978-1-59059-644-9

ISBN-10 (pbk): 1-59059-644-7

Printed and bound in the United States of America 9 8 7 6 5 4 3 2 1

Trademarked names may appear in this book. Rather than use a trademark symbol with every occurrence of a trademarked name, we use the names only in an editorial fashion and to the benefit of the trademark owner, with no intention of infringement of the trademark.

Lead Editor: Jonathan Hassell
Technical Reviewers: Srini Chavali, Sandra Vucinic
Editorial Board: Steve Anglin, Dan Appleman, Ewan Buckingham, Gary Cornell, Jason Gilmore, Jonathan Hassell, James Huddleston, Chris Mills, Matthew Moodie, Dominic Shakeshaft, Jim Sumser, Matt Wade
Project Manager: Elizabeth Seymour
Copy Edit Manager: Nicole LeClerc
Copy Editor: Andy Carroll
Assistant Production Director: Kari Brooks-Copony
Production Editor: Laura Cheu
Compositor: Dina Quan
Proofreader: Linda Seifert
Indexer: Carol Burbo
Artist: Kinetic Publishing Services, LLC
Photographer: Chris Fieldhouse
Cover Designer: Kurt Krames
Manufacturing Director: Tom Debolski

Distributed to the book trade worldwide by Springer-Verlag New York, Inc., 233 Spring Street, 6th Floor, New York, NY 10013. Phone 1-800-SPRINGER, fax 201-348-4505, e-mail orders-ny@springer-sbm.com, or visit http://www.springeronline.com.

For information on translations, please contact Apress directly at 2560 Ninth Street, Suite 219, Berkeley, CA 94710. Phone 510-549-5930, fax 510-549-5939, e-mail info@apress.com, or visit http://www.apress.com.

The information in this book is distributed on an "as is" basis, without warranty. Although every precaution has been taken in the preparation of this work, neither the author(s) nor Apress shall have any liability to any person or entity with respect to any loss or damage caused or alleged to be caused directly or indirectly by the information contained in this work.

Contents at a Glance

Contents

About the Authors

I am **Elke Phelps**. I started my work with Oracle products over 12 years ago with Oracle version 6. Until late 2000, my exposure to Oracle was as an Oracle DBA; I became an Oracle Certified Professional in 2000. My work as an Oracle Applications DBA began approximately 5 years ago. At first, it was a little overwhelming. The Oracle E-Business Suite is a *very* complex application. Not only does an Oracle Applications DBA assume the role of a database administrator, but many of us are also responsible for administering all of the components of the Oracle Applications Technology Stack including Oracle Developer, the Oracle Application Server, JInitiator, J2SE (JDK), and JDBC. I quickly found that there was no single reference for me to read to assist with my transition to being an Oracle Applications DBA. I started indexing commonly read Oracle documentation to assist me with my daily tasks. I also began developing a toolkit for managing Oracle Applications. The toolkit served as my library for looking up commonly used commands and information.

My involvement with the broader Oracle Applications user community began in the fall of 2004 when I presented at the Oracle Applications Users Groups (OAUG) conference, Connection Point, in Orlando (http:// www.oaug.org/). Based on feedback from this presentation, I was encouraged by OAUG board member, Mark Farnham to start a Special Interest Group (SIG) to address the Oracle Application Server as it related to the Oracle E-Business Suite. I expanded this idea to include all components of the Application Technology Stack and formed the Applications Technology Stack (ATS) SIG in February 2005. During the course of 2005, the objectives of the ATS SIG were extended to include additional middleware components. As part of the restructuring, we renamed the SIG as the Middleware SIG (http://mwsig.oaug.org/).

Presiding over the SIG has given me the opportunity to communicate with many Oracle Applications DBAs as well as other professionals who help support or use the Oracle E-Business Suite around the world. It was from this interaction that I became aware that many Oracle Applications DBAs were spending immeasurable amounts of time looking for basic information and commands to perform their jobs, just as I did. In mid-2005, I realized that it would be helpful if there were an Oracle Applications DBA reference guide, and that's when the idea to write the book was born. My primary objective in writing this guide was to provide a quick at-a-glance reference guide to assist other Oracle Applications DBAs in performing their day-to-day tasks. A web site maintained by Elke and Paul with additional information and tips for Oracle Applications can be found at http://www.fieldappsdba.com.

I am **Paul Jackson**, an Oracle Applications DBA with over 5 years' experience administering Human Resources and Financial modules. In this role, I have been actively involved in the user community, including serving as Program Director of the Middleware SIG (formerly the Applications Technology Stack SIG) and coauthoring multiple white papers. Prior to my involvement with Oracle Applications, I worked as an Oracle DBA and software developer.

Outside of work, I enjoy watching films, reading, and spending time with family and friends. By utilizing the proactive administration techniques outlined in this book, and working with very talented colleagues like Elke, I have time to pursue other interests like working out and playing poker.

About the Technical Reviewers

Sandra Vucinic has over 12 years of experience with Oracle database administration specifically supporting Oracle Applications environments including installation, implementations, administration, maintenance, upgrades, and remote support. Her focus is in areas of infrastructure planning, and architecture design, review, and support, with emphasis on Oracle Applications implementations and upgrades. In March of 2001, Sandra founded VLAD Group, Inc. (http://www.vladgroup.com), a woman-owned small business and a leading provider of expert-level resources to Fortune 1000 companies.

For years Sandra has been a presenter and panel member at Oracle Applications Users Group (OAUG), North Central OAUG, Central States OAUG, Southwest Regional OAUG, and Apps World and Open World conferences. For a fourth year, Sandra continues to serve on the board of directors for OAUG Database Special Interest Group (SIG) and OAUG SysAdmin SIG. In 2004 Sandra joined SouthWest Regional OAUG board as Secretary Director and Communications Director. Last year, Sandra accepted a position on OAUG Middleware SIG Leadership Team and serves as Membership Director. Sandra may be contacted at sandrav@vladgroup.com.

Srini Chavali has over 20 years of experience in the IT industry. He graduated from Osmania University, Hyderabad, India, with a bachelor's degree in chemical engineering and then completed his master's degree from the National Institute for Industrial Engineering in Mumbai (Bombay), India. He started his IT career with Tata Burroughs Ltd. (now part of Tata Consultancy Services) in Mumbai, India, which was a joint venture between India's Tata Group and the then Burroughs Corp. (which later became Unisys after its merger with Sperry Rand). Srini has had various IT roles, from consultant to developer to DBA to Applications DBA to manager, with Tata Burroughs, Liberty Travel (NJ), Toys"R"Us, AlliedSignal (now Honeywell), and is currently employed by Cummins Inc., Columbus, IN, as Manager of Technical Services.

Srini was introduced to the Oracle world while employed by Toys"R"Us in their corporate headquarters in New Jersey. Srini's team was supporting internal inventory and sales systems based on mainframes, and he was part of the team that started the migration of those systems to an Oracle-based version. After joining Cummins in 1998, Srini started working with Oracle Applications versions 10.4 and 10.7. He is the technical lead of the implementations of Financial and HR modules (versions 11.5.5 through 11.5.10) at Cummins. His team now also provides technical best practices on all of the Applications modules to the various Manufacturing Applications installations and upgrades at the many Cummins plants worldwide.

Srini resides in Indianapolis, IN, and is married and has one daughter.

Acknowledgments

There are many people that I would like to thank for their support and encouragement. First, to my parents, Brigitte and Jerry, thank you for providing me a loving home and for encouraging and enabling me to pursue my dreams. To my sisters, Susanna and especially Karin (who was my rock in my early college years), thank you for your love and support. I owe a special token of gratitude to my Oma, Gerda, for instilling in me a strong work ethic and teaching me the meaning of courage. Thanks to Phil for not only being the best boss that I ever had, but for being my friend and mentor. Thanks to Glenn for sharing with me his ability to listen, his calm demeanor, and his wisdom—I still have much to learn from his examples. Silly as it may sound, thanks to my cats, Thelonious, Georgie, and Crouton for "helping" me type and burn the midnight oil. A special thanks to my colleague and coauthor, Paul, for listening to my idea of writing this guide and for helping me see it through to publication. Last, but not least, to my husband Richard, thank you for your encouragement, your patience, and your love. I would not be who or where I am today without you in my life.

Elke

First and foremost I would like to thank my parents, Paul and Mary Ann, for all of their love and encouragement. Many heartfelt thanks to my aunt, Lynn Griffin for her enthusiasm about the project. I would like to extend additional thanks to Janine Hempy and her dog Booger, Kevin Barnes, David Skelton, Jason Driver, and too many others to mention. I owe much for the support provided by all of these people. Finally, I would like to acknowledge my colleague and friend, Elke for her dedication to this project. Without her vision and hard work, you would not be reading this book today.

Paul

We would both like to extend a *BIG* thank you to the guide's technical reviewers, Srini and Sandra. A book is only as good as its technical reviewers. We had the pleasure of having two of the leaders in the Oracle Applications user community share in the endeavor of this publication. Srini and Sandra, thank you for taking the time and energy required to assist us in getting this guide published.

xvi ■ ACKNOWLEDGMENTS

would also like to extend a special thank you to our initial editor
Tony Davis. Tony helped us in so many ways. He assisted us in landing the
book deal with Apress and in setting the tone for the guide very early in the
writing process. If you like the way the book reads, that is due in large part
to the guidance we received from Tony.

There is a large team of people who spent many long hours working to
get this guide to print. We would like to thank lead editor, Jonathan Hassell,
our project manager, Elizabeth Seymour, our copy editor, Andy Carroll, our
production editor, Laura Cheu, and the rest of the Apress team that helped
with the publication of this guide.

We would also like to thank the Oracle Applications Users Group and
the rest of Middleware SIG Leadership Team (Andrea and Adrienne) for their
continued support and dedication. To the Oracle Applications user community, thank you for giving us the opportunity to serve you. This book is for
you. We hope that you find it beneficial.

Elke and Paul

Introduction

The Oracle E-Business Suite is like a machine that requires constant maintenance and fine-tuning. With experience comes the knowledge of how to tweak the parts and use the tools to make it run properly. Even for the experienced administrator, Oracle Applications is complicated to administer—let's be honest, at times it can be a real headache. Making this task even more difficult is the need to search through numerous MetaLink notes and references, Oracle's online Electronic Technical Reference Manuals (eTRMs), and other published works for the how-to of daily tasks. As with most trades, there are hidden secrets that are uncovered only through experience or trial and error.

After many arduous years of searching for information in Oracle's online documentation, and resolving unexpected errors, we decided to work towards sparing other Oracle Applications DBAs the same fate. Many of the tips in *Oracle Applications DBA Field Guide* are unpublished essentials that will benefit every Oracle Applications DBA.

It is impossible to provide in-depth details for this complex system in a small reference manual; however, the objective of this guide is to provide the most critical information required to provide a stable, proactively managed system. This guide provides the tools and insight an Oracle Applications DBA or an Oracle E-Business Suite customer needs to understand the complexities of the system and the best practices associated with maintaining it. The subject matter covered in this guide is intended to be independent of the specific modules available in Oracle Applications, and it does assume that you have some knowledge of database and open systems architecture.

Oracle Applications DBA Field Guide is a toolkit containing scripts, notes, references, and guidelines developed by experienced Oracle Applications DBAs to administer the E-Business Suite. It contains proven tips and techniques on topics ranging from architecture, configuration, monitoring and troubleshooting, performance tuning, and patching. Also provided in the guide are best practices for administering Oracle Applications. All of this information is provided in a format that is easy to read and quick to navigate. As such, it will serve as a useful supplement to the existing documentation for Oracle E-Business Suite.

■ ■ ■

## CHAPTER 1

Components and Architecture of Oracle Applications

The Oracle E-Business Suite is a complex Enterprise Resource Planning program that consists of many components. The primary components that comprise the E-Business Suite are the Client, Forms Server, Web Server, Concurrent Processor, and Oracle Database. Each of these plays a role in servicing Oracle Applications.

This chapter will provide an overview of the function that each of these components provides to enable end-users to access and use the application. We'll look at two main topics in this chapter:

- **Oracle Applications**: An overview of how users access the applications and the different components that service their requests. In the process, we'll look briefly at the Client, Web Node, Forms Node, Concurrent Processing Node, and Database Node.

- **Oracle Applications architecture**: A look at the architecture of the E-Business Suite from basic to complex configurations. This includes load balancing nodes, a shared APPL_TOP or Application Tier Filesystem, distributed APPL_TOP, and Secure Socket Layer (SSL) Encryption.

In addition to the primary components identified so far, there are many other components of the E-Business Suite architecture, including networking infrastructure, servers, routers, and load balancing devices, to mention only a few.

■Note While we will provide an overview of complex, advanced architecture infrastructures, the details of how to implement one are beyond the scope of this guide. Oracle Discoverer, Oracle Portal, Oracle Internet Directory, Oracle Single Sign-on, Oracle Web Cache, and Oracle Integration are also out of the scope of this guide.

Servicing User Requests—Oracle Applications Components

In order to understand the primary components of the Oracle E-Business Suite, it is important to know how the user accesses the application. As the first step to accessing Oracle Applications, a user will launch a web browser and enter the URL that is the *web entry point* for the application. The Web Server then services the access request.

The first page that is displayed by the Web Server is a login screen. Once logged in, the user picks a responsibility, such as System Administrator, and then a menu option, such as Security : User ➤ Define, to begin his or her work. The menu option will direct the user to an HTML or JavaServer Pages (JSP) page, or to a Forms application. The Web Server will continue to service HTML or Java servlet requests; however, if a Forms application is launched, a Forms servlet or the Forms Server will service it. Throughout this process, the user is retrieving data and executing packages from within the Oracle Database.

Now that you have a very high-level overview of how users access the application, we can look at some specifics of the components that service requests. The following components will be described:

- **Client**: The requirements and processes on the user workstation

- **Web Node**: Web Server processes that run on the Web Node

- **Forms Node**: Forms Server processes that run on the Forms Node

- **Concurrent Processing Node**: Concurrent Manager processes running on the Concurrent Processing Node

- **Admin Node**: Administrative tasks executed on the Admin Node

- **Database Node**: Database services that run on the Database Node

---

■**Note** A node comprises processing power (CPU) and memory. Multiple nodes servicing different functions may be hosted on the same server. For example, a Web Node, Forms Node, Concurrent Processing Node, and Admin Node may all run on the same Oracle Application Server.

Client

Users accessing Oracle Applications are required to have an Oracle-certified web browser, such as Microsoft Internet Explorer or Netscape. Oracle Applications are served as either web applications or Oracle Forms. A user's first interaction with the application is a login screen that is presented in the web browser, and from there the user can either continue to access web pages or can access Forms applications. The Oracle JInitiator plug-in is required to run Oracle Forms as Java applets on the Client.

Web Node

The user initially accesses the application via a web browser with a URL for the web entry point. The Web Server services this web page request. For Oracle applications, the Web Server is the Oracle Application Server, which is based on Apache technology, and the Web Node is the node that runs this server. The Oracle Application Server is also called iAS, AS, Oracle HTTP Server (OHS), or simply Apache.

The iAS listens for incoming requests on a specific port. The iAS also runs the JServs that are used to service Java requests. For Oracle Applications, the iAS may also be configured to run Forms servlets. If this is the case, then the iAS will also service Forms sessions.

Forms Node

If Forms servlets are not configured for the iAS, then Forms sessions are serviced by the Forms Server. When a Forms request is initiated, the iAS hands off the Forms request to the Forms Server. Much like the iAS, the Forms Server listens for incoming requests on a specific port. The Forms Node is the node that runs the Forms Server.

Concurrent Processing Node

Concurrent processing is a special feature of Oracle Applications. It allows the user to schedule jobs, which Oracle calls *requests*. These requests may be standard Oracle requests or custom requests, they can be scheduled as one-time requests or on a repeating schedule, and they can be submitted to execute immediately or at a specific time.

Requests are scheduled with the scheduling manager, which is called the *Concurrent Manager*. The node that runs the Concurrent Manager processes is called the Concurrent Processing Node.

Admin Node

There are many administrative tasks that are executed in order to maintain the Oracle E-Business Suite, such as regenerating forms, regenerating jar files, applying application patches, and recompiling flexfields. The Admin Node is used to execute administrative tasks.

Database Node

The heart and soul of the E-Business Suite is the database. The database not only stores the data in tables under various schemas, but also stores many other objects (such as procedures, packages, database triggers, functions, indexes, and sequences) that are required for the application to function. The Database Node is where the Oracle Database instance runs and accesses the database files.

Oracle Applications Architecture

Some implementations of Oracle Applications are set up with a basic configuration. Others require advanced configuration for specific features. We will start with an overview of the basic architecture requirements and then move into advanced configuration options.

Fundamental Architecture

When a system is deployed with a basic approach to architecture, it typically does not have large transactional processing requirements or a large concurrent user base. For this environment, there are no special configuration requirements. These implementations may run on one tier, meaning that all nodes are running on one physical server, but this is a very inefficient method.

Some implementations run the application components on one server, while the database node runs on a separate server. This is a *two-tier architecture*. Multi-tier environments do not require special configuration or design effort unless multiple nodes for the same component are required (this will be described in greater detail in the following "Advanced Architecture" section). A simple, two-tier Oracle Applications environment is displayed in Figure 1-1.

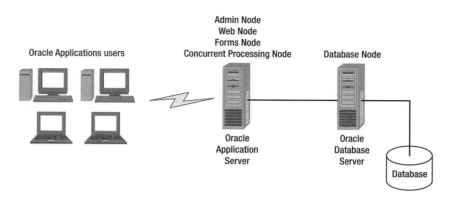

Figure 1-1. *Oracle applications: two-tier architecture*

Traditionally, Oracle recommended that the Concurrent Processing Node run the same tier as the Database Node. However, with fast network connectivity between the Concurrent Processing Node and the Database Node, it is now recommended that the Concurrent Processing Node run on the application tier.

■**Tip** A two-tier architecture is the minimum number of tiers recommended to run Oracle Applications. Single-tier architectures can cause contention between application and database processing, which will result in performance degradation.

Advanced Architecture

When more nodes of the application tier are split across multiple servers, and additional nodes are defined for the same component, we begin to enter into advanced configuration topics and design.

Advanced, multi-tier configurations for Oracle Applications include combining multiple Web, Forms, Concurrent Processing, and Database Nodes. The number of nodes required is dependent upon your environmental requirements for concurrent user support and transactional processing. An advanced multi-tiered Oracle Applications environment is displayed in Figure 1-2:

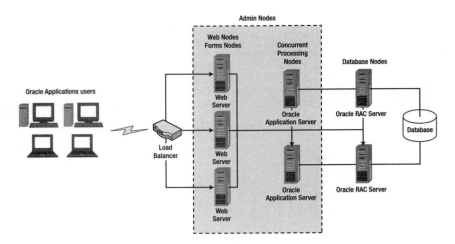

Figure 1-2. *Oracle Applications: an advanced multi-tier architecture*

This section will not provide the details required to implement a complex architecture, but it will give you the background to begin research into which advanced configuration topologies might be required by the organization you service. The following topics will be covered in this section:

- **Load balancing**: The requirements for load balancing the various nodes of the E-Business Suite

- **Shared APPL_TOP or Application Tier Filesystem**: The support of a shared applications layer, and when it should be used

- **Distributed APPL_TOP**: The support of a distributed application layer, and when it is beneficial

- **Secure Sockets Layer (SSL) Encryption**: An overview of SSL and its implementation requirements for Oracle Applications

Load Balancing

When a large number of users need to access your environment, or when the number of transactions to be processed is great, it may be necessary to create multiple nodes that service the same function. For example, if your business or customer requires the ability to support 5,000 concurrent Forms users, servicing these requests with either one Web Node or one Forms Server may cause contention in the system. This would result in users being unable to access the application. In order to resolve this problem, multiple Web or Forms Nodes would need to be put into operation.

Load balancing is the term used to describe how users or transactions are distributed to multiple nodes that service the same function. When more than one node is used, the nodes that service the same function are called a *farm*. For example, if you determine that your environment requires multiple Web Nodes, the multiple Web Nodes are collectively referred to as a *Web farm*. The Web Nodes may be further load balanced by implementing multiple JServs per Web Server. If your environment requires a large amount of Java processing, configuring additional JServs will reduce contention for its resources.

Web Node load balancing may be achieved by employing a hardware load balancing device or with DNS load balancing. Forms load balancing is implemented with either the Web Node as the load balancer for Forms servlets or as multiple Forms Nodes. If multiple Forms Nodes are implemented, one of the Web Nodes is designated as the primary Web Node and serves as the entry point for access to the Forms Nodes. The Forms Metrics Server runs on the primary Web Node and serves as the load balancer for sending requests to the multiple Forms Nodes. Information regarding advanced configuration for the Oracle E-Business Suite can be found in MetaLink Note 217368.1.

When the Concurrent Processing Nodes are load balanced, this configuration is referred to as *Parallel Concurrent Processing*. Parallel Concurrent Processing is load balanced by the Internal Concurrent Manager. If Parallel Concurrent Processing is required, then a shared filesystem implemented with either Network Filesystem (NFS) or a shared disk array is required to share log and output files that are generated by the Concurrent Managers. Additional information regarding Parallel Concurrent Processing may be found in MetaLink Note 185489.1.

For the database, a multiple-node implementation may be achieved by implementing Oracle Real Application Clusters (RAC). In a RAC environment, multiple Database Nodes function as one database instance, accessing the same database files. Additional information for implementing Oracle RAC with 11i may be found in MetaLink Note 312731.1.

■**Note** Oracle has not certified and does not support load balancing of the same types of nodes on the same physical server.

Shared APPL_TOP or Application Tier Filesystem

Each implementation of Oracle Applications contains an APPL_TOP and a COMMON_TOP directory on each node. The APPL_TOP directory comprises all product files and directories, all core technology files and directories, as well as the application context file and environment files. Details regarding the context file and environment files are provided in Chapter 2 of this guide. The COMMON_TOP directory contains files and directories that are used by all application products.

While not necessary, it is recommended that you investigate implementing a shared APPL_TOP or Application Tier Filesystem for a multiple-node installation. In a shared APPL_TOP implementation, a shared filesystem (either NFS or a disk array) is used to store the APPL_TOP and COMMON_TOP structures. Because the APPL_TOP and COMMON_TOP directories contain application code and binaries, placing them on a shareable filesystem will reduce maintenance downtime, since only one copy of the APPL_TOP and COMMON_TOP sources exist.

As of version 11.5.10 of Oracle Applications, a shared Application Tier Filesystem may be implemented. A shared Application Tier Filesystem not only includes the APPL_TOP and COMMON_TOP directories, but also the Applications Technology Stack components of the iAS and Developer Tools (Forms, Reports) installation. This provides even greater manageability of the application environment.

Just imagine having an implementation on ten nodes without a shared APPL_TOP or Application Tier Filesystem. You would need to maintain the application and Applications Technology Stack code for all ten nodes! This exemplifies the benefit of a Shared APPL_TOP or Application Tier Filesystem. MetaLink Note 233428.1 provides details for implementing a shared APPL_TOP or Application Tier Filesystem.

Distributed APPL_TOP

A distributed APPL_TOP is yet another advanced configuration feature of Oracle Applications. With this configuration, you can use some or all of the servers in your implementation to serve as Admin Nodes. An administrative task will distribute workers on multiple servers that are configured as Admin Nodes.

This feature may assist in reducing downtime by expediting administrative functions, such as when a patching session spawns multiple workers across multiple nodes. Details for implementing a distributed APPL_TOP are outlined in MetaLink Note 236469.1.

Secure Sockets Layer Encryption

Secure Sockets Layer (SSL) is a method of encrypting transactions and data over a network. Securing transactional data is often a requirement when said transactions contain sensitive data or information, such as credit card data.

If encryption is required, it may be implemented with Oracle Applications. SSL may be implemented for the Oracle HTTP Server, Forms Server, and Database Server. SSL may be implemented with software or with a hardware device known as an SSL accelerator. Details for implementing SSL are given in MetaLink Note 123718.1.

Architecture Best Practices

When designing the infrastructure of your Oracle E-Business Suite implementation, it is important to understand your service level agreement with the customer, as well as the concurrent user requirements of the application. This will help you determine the level of scalability and availability that you will need to provide. Additional scalability and availability may be achieved by implementing multiple nodes that service the same function.

If you are considering implementing multiple nodes for load balancing, it is recommended that you consider implementing the additional nodes on commodity servers. Commodity servers are cheaper servers generally based on the Intel architecture running Linux. Implementing commodity servers will allow you to transition to a load balanced, multi-tier configuration with a lower total cost of ownership.

While details regarding implementing Oracle Web Cache were not discussed in this chapter, it is worth investigating this technology as part of your E-Business architecture solution. Overall performance may be significantly improved if Oracle Web Cache is implemented with your environment. Additional details regarding implementing Web Cache may be found in MetaLink Note 306653.1.

Infrastructure upgrade requirements, including client workstation, server, networking, and hardware firmware upgrades, to mention a few, should be implemented with caution. A "minor" upgrade to one of these components may cause outages for your Oracle Applications environment. Be certain to sufficiently test all such upgrades or modifications to the supporting Oracle E-Business Suite infrastructure, and have a plan to roll back changes if necessary.

■ ■ ■

## CHAPTER 2

Configuration

In order to administer the Oracle E-Business Suite, it is important to have a thorough understanding of Oracle Applications configuration. According to Oracle, approximately 60 percent of all logged issues are configuration related. Although Oracle has attempted to automate much of the configuration management, an Oracle Applications DBA still needs to be familiar with the files and settings of the application. Without this knowledge, managing and troubleshooting issues is all the more difficult. This chapter will discuss key aspects of configuring the application and the tools used to do so. This chapter assumes that you have already enabled AD Configuration, also known as autoconfig, for your environment, and provides tips for using it once it is configured.

■Note For information on how to enable AD Configuration, see MetaLink Note 218089.1.

This chapter will cover the following topics:

- **Application context file**: This file contains settings that apply to the whole Oracle E-Business Suite. We will look at how to define, locate, build, and maintain the application context file, and at a recommended method for port numbering for ease of application administration.

- **Using AD Configuration**: The AD Configuration utility can be used to automate configuration of the application and database tiers. We'll discuss how template files are utilized by AD Configuration, how to review and compare the execution of autoconfig, how to locate the autoconfig execution log files, and where to locate the autoconfig backup files.

- **Web Node configuration:** This section will cover the key configuration files, and their most important parameters, for managing the Oracle Application Server, such as the httpd.conf, jserv.conf, jserv.properties, zone.properties, ssp_init.txt, and wdbsvr.app files, and the session.timeout setting.

- **Forms Node configuration:** This section will cover key configuration files and parameters for managing the Forms Server. We'll also provide an overview of how to load balance Forms traffic using the Forms Metric Server and Forms Metric Client.

- **Concurrent Processing Node configuration:** In this section, we'll discuss the key configuration files and parameters for managing the Concurrent Processing Node and for configuring both the listener process used by this node and the Report Review Agent (FNDFS).

- **Admin Node configuration:** The Admin Node is used to perform administrative functions and configuration. In this section, we'll discuss application environment files, the location of administrative scripts, creating the identity.obj file, configuring the database connection (DBC) file, setting and validating the CLASSPATH, and configuring the Generic Service Management (GSM).

- **Additional service components:** In this section, we'll cover secondary service components including TCF Socket, Discoverer Server, and the JTF Fulfillment Server.

- **Database Node configuration:** This section will cover recommended settings for database version 9*i* and 10*g* initialization parameters for optimum performance with Oracle Applications 11*i*. We'll also outline how to set up and test remote database connectivity with the listener.ora and tnsnames.ora files. This section also includes an overview of the Oracle Applications Tablespace Model (OATM), and tips and conventions for creating custom database objects.

- **Additional configuration topics:** This section will discuss how to use features of Oracle Applications Manager (OAM) to implement advanced configuration with the configuration wizards, and to review and license products. We'll also provide tips for enhancing application and database security. Finally, we'll provide an overview of managing the oraInst.loc and oratab files, and a few miscellaneous context file parameters.

The Application Context File

The nodes that comprise Oracle Applications have numerous configuration files, and administering these files can be quite cumbersome. In order to improve the management of the configuration files, Oracle has created a common file that stores values for many of the configuration settings for all components of the E-Business Suite. This global application configuration file is called the *application context file* or the *application XML file*.

Locating and Creating the Application Context File

The application context file is an XML file named $CONTEXT_NAME.xml. The CONTEXT_NAME variable is set to $SID or $SID_[hostname]. The application context file is located in the $APPL_TOP/admin directory, and it is applicable to all nodes that comprise the E-Business Suite.

If the application context file does not exist, it can be created by executing the adbldxml.sh script:

```
$ ./$AD_TOP/bin/adbldxml.sh
```

This script will evaluate your environment in order to generate the context file. A directory listing should confirm the existence of this application context file.

Modifying the Application Context File

Once the application context file has been created, there are several ways to edit it:

- Using editcontext
- Using OAM
- Using a standard text editor

Using editcontext

Oracle recommends using the editcontext utility, which provides a GUI interface for editing the XML file. The drawbacks to using editcontext are that it requires X-emulation software to run, and it is quite cumbersome to use because the parameters are not listed in any logical sequence. As a result, it is sometimes difficult to find the exact parameter that needs to be modified.

To use the `editcontext` utility, execute the following commands:

```
$ export DISPLAY=myclient:0.0
$ cd $COMMON_TOP/util/editcontext
$ ./editcontext
```

■**Note** The DISPLAY must be set to the client where the X-emulation software is executed.

Using OAM

Another Oracle-supported method for editing the application context file is to use Oracle Applications Manager (OAM). OAM offers a user-friendly, searchable interface for modifying the context file. OAM also offers the ability to save and recover context file versions as well as display differences between versions of context files.

To edit the context file in OAM, click on Sitemap ➤ Context File Parameters. The parameters on the Context File Parameters screen are ordered by tabs that categorize the parameters in the file. The tabs are Global, System, Local, Install, Environments, Processes, and Custom as shown in Figure 2-1.

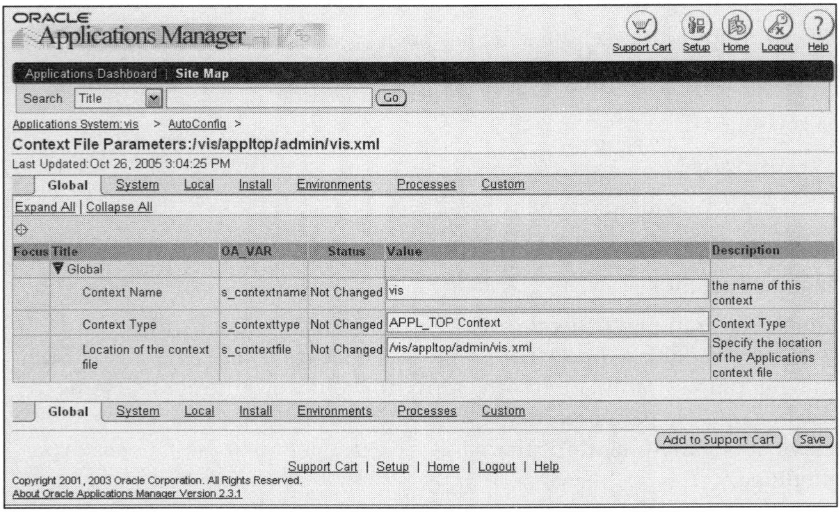

Figure 2-1. *Using OAM to edit the application context file*

Using a Standard Text Editor

The application context file may also be edited manually with a standard text editor, such as `vi`. Here's an example:

```
$ cd $APPL_TOP/admin
$ vi VIS_MYSERVER.xml
```

Due to the possibility for human error, you should make a backup copy of the context file before editing in this manner. When creating a backup of the context file, it is helpful to use a date-based extension, such as `$CONTEXT_NAME.xml.yymmdd`.

Tip Editing the context file with a text editor such as `vi` should only be performed by experienced Oracle Applications DBAs.

Creating a Port Numbering Convention

The settings defined in the context file include many port numbers. Oracle provides some default port numbers in the basic configuration, but if multiple instances of Oracle Applications are running on the same server, a port numbering convention can simplify instance management.

Oracle provides 100 port pools to allow for multiple instances on the same server. MetaLink Note 216664.1 includes a table that calculates port values for any valid Port Pool value of 0 through 99. Essentially, the Port Pool value is added to the default port value in order to create a unique port number.

Rather than using port pools, the Oracle Applications DBA can create a customized port numbering scheme. For example, you could place all ports for one instance within a range of 500 possible values, such as 19000–19500. For the next instance, all values could be incremented by 500. Table 2-1 shows an example port numbering convention for two test instances.

Table 2-1. *An Example Port Numbering Convention for Two Test Instances*

Port Description	Context File Parameter	Default	Test 1 Port	Test 2 Port
Database	s_dbport	1521	19000	19500
Reports	s_repsport	7000	19005	19505
Web Listener	s_webport	8000	19010	19510
Oprocmgr	s_oprocmgrport	8100	19015	19515
Web PLSQL	s_webport_pls	8200	19020	19520
Servlet	s_servletport	8800	19025	19525
Forms Listener	s_formsport	9000	19030	19530
Metric Server Data	s_metdataport	9100	19035	19535
Metric Server Request	s_metreqport	9200	19040	19540
JTF Fulfillment Server	s_jtfuf_port	9300	19045	19545
Map Viewer Servlet	s_mapviewer_port	9800	19050	19550
OEM Web Utility	s_oemweb_port	10000	19055	19555
VisiBroker OrbServer Agent	s_osagent_port	10100	19060	19560
MSCA Server	s_mwaPortNo	10200	19065	19565
MSCA Dispatcher	s_mwaDispatcherPort	10300	19070	19570
OACORE Servlet Range	s_oacore_servlet_portrange	16000-16009	19101-19110	19601-19610
Discoverer Servlet Range	s_disco_servlet_portrange	17000-17009	19111-19120	19611-19620
Forms Servlet Range	s_forms_servlet_portrange	18000-18009	19121-19130	19621-19630
XMLSVCS Servlet Range	s_xmlsvcs_servlet_portrange	19000-19009	19131-19140	19631-19640

Prior to selecting a port, the UNIX netstat and grep commands can be used to verify that the port is not already in use on the server. If netstat returns rows for the port, then the port is in use. The following example tests whether or not port 19000 is being used:

```
$ netstat -a | grep 19000
```

```
tcp4 0 0 *.19000 *.* LISTEN
tcp4 0 0 dbserver.19000 client.55555 ESTABLISHED
```

In this case, port 19000 is already in use. The LISTEN section of the output shows that a service is listening on port 19000, while the ESTABLISHED section indicates that a connection has been established to port 19000 by a client.

■**Tip** It is good practice to update the /etc/services file on the server with all services that require ports. This assists in documenting port allocation for the server.

Identifying Nodes with Context Parameters

Nodes are of the following types: Database, Admin, Web, Forms, or Concurrent Processing. There are several parameters within the context file that are used to identify the type of node, and the AD utilities will use these parameters to perform tasks such as creating control scripts or maintaining necessary files to support services.

For multi-node installations with separate APPL_TOPs, each node's context file will need to specify the appropriate type for that node. If a shared APPL_TOP is used, all parameters will need to be set to yes, because that APPL_TOP is used by all nodes with the exception of the Database Node.

Table 2-2 lists the node-related parameters as of Oracle Applications 11.5.10.

Table 2-2. *Node-Identifying Context Parameters*

Context File Parameter	Description
s_isDB	Identifies node as a Database Node for autoconfig to create control scripts
s_isAdmin	Identifies node as an Admin Node for autoconfig to create control scripts
s_isWeb	Identifies node as a Web Node for autoconfig to create control scripts

Continued

Table 2-2. *Continued*

Context File Parameter	Description
s_isForms	Identifies node as a Forms Node for autoconfig to create control scripts
s_isConc	Identifies node as a Concurrent Processing Node for autoconfig to create control scripts
s_isAdadmin	Identifies node's APPL_TOP as being used to support the Oracle Applications system
s_isAdWeb	Identifies node's APPL_TOP as being used to support Web services
s_isAdForms	Identifies node's APPL_TOP as being used to support Forms services
s_isAdConc	Identifies node's APPL_TOP as being used to support Concurrent Processing services

Using AD Configuration

When modifications have been made to the context file, or when post-patch-step requirements dictate (patching will be discussed in Chapter 5 of this guide), the AD Configuration utility needs be executed on all nodes in order to implement the configuration changes.

Executing AD Configuration

The AD Configuration utility, adconfig.sh (also known as autoconfig) can be executed against all nodes of Oracle Applications, including the Database Node. The file adconfig.sh and all of its supporting scripts are located in the $AD_TOP/bin directory.

Templates are used by AD Configuration to change all configuration files for the different nodes. Patches to the Rapid Install product, also known as ADX, update the templates and the parameters in the XML file. All application processes should be shut down prior to executing adconfig.sh.

The adconfig.sh command will prompt for the location of the context file and the APPS password. As of version 11.5.10, Oracle introduced the adautocfg.sh script in the $COMMON_TOP/admin/scripts/$CONTEXT_NAME directory to serve as a wrapper to adconfig.sh. When executing adautocfg.sh, the location of the context file is not required.

To execute the AD Configuration utility, you would use a command like this:

```
$ ./$AD_TOP/bin/adconfig.sh \
contextfile=$APPLTOP/admin/$CONTEXT_NAME.xml \
appspass=password
```

If you are calling `adautocfg.sh` from the application tier, the command would look like this:

```
$ ./$COMMON_TOP/admin/scripts/$CONTEXT_NAME/adautocfg.sh
```

■Tip If configuration files are modified manually, you will need to edit the context file to keep the settings synchronized; otherwise, changes to the underlying configuration file will be overwritten the next time AD Configuration (`adconfig.sh`) is executed.

Reviewing adconfig.sh Log Files

The execution of `adconfig.sh` generates a log file. You should review the log file for any errors that may exist and work to resolve them.

The log file for the execution of `adconfig.sh` on the application tier is located here, where `MM` is the month, `DD` is the day, `hh` is the hour, and `mm` is the minute when `adconfig.sh` was executed:

```
$APPL_TOP/admin/$CONTEXT_NAME/log/MMDDhhmm/adconfig.log
```

The log file for the execution of `adconfig.sh` on the database tier located here, with `MMDDhhmm` having the same meaning:

```
$ORACLE_HOME/appsutil/log/$CONTEXT_NAME/MMDDhhmm/adconfig.log
```

Reviewing adconfig.sh Execution Changes

If you want to determine configuration changes that will be made by executing `adconfig.sh`, you can execute the `adchkcfg.sh` script. This script generates an HTML file named `cfgcheck.html` that displays the differences in the configurations.

The HTML file is located in the following directory on the application tier, where MM is the month, DD is the day, hh is the hour, and mm is the minute when adchkcfg.sh was executed:

$APPL_TOP/admin/$CONTEXT_NAME/out/MMDDhhmm

The cfgcheck.html file is located in the following directory on the database tier, with MMDDhhmm having the same meaning:

$ORACLE_HOME/appsutil/log/$CONTEXT_NAME/out/MMDDhhmm

Location of adconfig.sh Backup Files

The execution of adconfig.sh generates backup files.

The backup files for the execution of adconfig.sh on the application tier are located in the following directory, where MM is the month, DD is the day, hh is the hour, and mm is the minute when adconfig.sh was executed:

$APPL_TOP/admin/$CONTEXT_NAME/out/MMDDhhmm

The backup files for the execution of adconfig.sh on the database tier are located in the following directory, with MMDDhhmm having the same meaning:

$ORACLE_HOME/appsutil/log/$CONTEXT_NAME/out/MMDDhhmm

■**Tip** If you want to restore configuration files from the backup of an adconfig.sh run, you can execute the $APPL_TOP/admin/$CONTEXT_NAME/out/MMDDhhmm/restore.sh script. On the database server, this script will be found in the $ORACLE_HOME/ appsutil/out/$CONTEXT_NAME/MMDDhhmm directory.

Adding Customizations to the Application Configuration Files

At times, it is necessary to add custom parameters and environment variables to a configuration file that are not stored within the parameters of the application's context file. This can be accomplished in two ways:

- Adding customization tags to configuration files or autoconfig templates
- Using OAM to add customizations

Adding Customization Tags to Configuration or Template Files

Prior to ADX minipack version F, the # Begin customization and # End customization tags can be added to the configuration file to support customizations. Customizations can be added by manually editing the application configuration files with a standard text editor.

Here is an example of using customizations by editing the adovars.env application configuration file:

```
# Begin customizations
# The SCRIPT_TOP environment variable is used for ease of navigation
# to the startup and shutdown scripts of the application
SCRIPT_TOP=/vis/applcomn/admin/scripts/VIS
export SCRIPT_TOP
# End customizations
```

■**Tip** The AD Configuration utility, when it is executed, will preserve customizations that are marked with customization tags. If customization tags are not used, the customizations will be removed. Be sure to use comments to document the purpose of your customizations.

With later versions of autoconfig, manual customizations should be implemented by using a custom template instead of adding tags to each configuration file. In order to migrate any customization tags from the manual configuration files to the custom template, the adcustomizer.sh script should be run on the node where the customizations have been made. The AD Configuration utility will then apply customizations that are in the custom template upon subsequent executions.

Adding Customizations Using Oracle Applications Manager

The Oracle Applications Manager (OAM) utility is able to support customization changes provided that the version used is later than minipack H. This feature can be accessed from the Site Map menu by selecting Administration ➤ AutoConfig ➤ Manage Custom Parameters. Clicking the Add button will allow you to create a custom parameter. Figure 2-2 shows the options for creating a new custom parameter for the Admin Node.

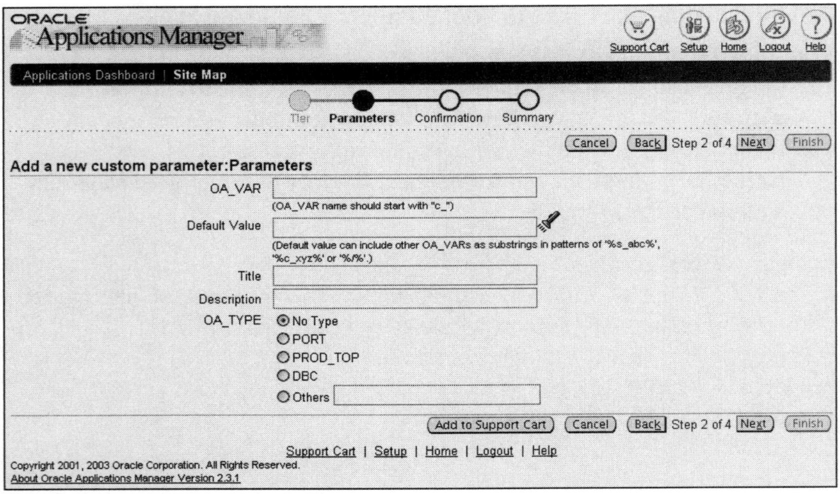

Figure 2-2. *OAM screen for adding custom parameters*

Web Node Configuration

Although most of the configuration is handled by the AD Configuration utility, it is important to be aware of the key configuration files for the Web Node. Sometimes it is necessary to change log levels and debug levels in these configuration files during troubleshooting.

The primary configuration files for web configuration are located in the $APACHE_TOP/Apache/conf and $APACHE_TOP/Jserv/etc directories. Additional configuration files are located under other subdirectories of $APACHE_TOP.

Apache Configuration Files

Apache configuration files identify port definitions, memory settings, logging levels, log file locations, and other configuration options. When the web server is started, a process identification (pid) file will be created in a directory described in the httpd.conf file. Key parameter settings in the httpd.conf file are shown in Table 2-3.

Table 2-3. *Key Parameters in the* httpd.conf *File*

Context File Parameter	Parameter in httpd.conf	Example Value	Description
s_web_pid_file	PidFile	/\<apache_top>/Apache/logs/httpd.pid	Location of file containing process ID for web server
s_minspare_servers	MinSpareServers	5	Minimum number of idle processes required
s_maxspare_servers	MaxSpareServers	10	Maximum number of idle processes allowed
s_webport	Port	19010	Port the server is listening on
s_webhost	ServerName	webserver.domain.com	Location of web server
s_apache_loglevel	LogLevel	Error	Level at which log messages are written
s_maxclients	MaxClients	1024	Number of concurrent client requests allowed

Another important configuration file, wdbsvr.app, is located in the $APACHE_TOP/modplsql/cfg directory. By default, the apps password is hard-coded inside the file. Details on changing and encrypting the apps password will be provided in Chapter 6 of this guide.

JServ Configuration Files

Configuration files required for the JServs can be found in the $APACHE_TOP/Jserv/etc directory. The primary configuration files in this directory are jserv.conf, jserv.properties, and zone.properties, and the key parameter settings in these files are shown in Tables 2-4 through 2-6.

Table 2-4. *Key Parameters in the* `jserv.conf` *File*

Context File Parameter	Parameter in jserv.conf	Example Value	Description
s_apjservloglevel	ApJServLogLevel	Error	Level at which log messages are written
s_hostname	ApJServDefaultHost	webserver. domain.com	Location of web server
s_oacore_nprocs	apJServGroup	X Y /\<apache_top>/ OACoreGroupJserv/ etc/jserv. properties	Used to configure multiple JServs, where X is the number of JServs to run and Y is the node weight. Node weight is used if multiple JServs are load balanced across multiple servers.

Table 2-5. *Key Parameters in the* `jserv.properties` *File*

Context File Parameter	Parameter in jserv.properties	Example Value	Description
s_jvm_options	wrapper.bin. parameters	-Xmx512M -Xms128M	Heap memory settings: mx is the maximum memory allowed and ms is the minimum memory required
s_fnd_secure	wrapper.bin. parameters= DJTFDBCFILE	/\<fnd_top>/ secure/ \<context_name>. dbc	Location of DBC file
s_display	wrapper.env=DISPLAY	\<xserver>:0.0	Location of X Windows server
s_webhost+s_ webentrydomain	Bindadress	Webserver. domain.com	Location of web server

Context File Parameter	Parameter in jserv.properties	Example Value	Description
s_oacore_servlet_ portrange	Port	19101-19110	Port number range
s_security_ maxconnections	security. maxConnections	50	Maximum number of socket connections JServ can handle simultaneously
s_oacorelog	Log	False	Indicates whether the JServ logs information

Table 2-6. *Key Parameters in the* zone.properties *File*

Context File Parameter	Parameter in zone.properties	Example Value	Description
s_sesstimeout	session.timeout	1800000	Time in milliseconds before web session times out

■**Tip** In order for session timeout to function properly, the session.timeout setting in the zone.properties file must match the application profile option ICX: Session Timeout. The session timeout value should not exceed 30 minutes. Values greater than 30 could result in JVM heap memory problems.

Forms Node Configuration

As with the Web Node, it is important for the Applications DBA to be familiar with the files and settings used by the Forms Node. This section will cover topics related to the basic configuration and some advanced configuration options.

Basic Configuration

All Forms application processing is handled by the Oracle Forms Server. The key configuration values in the $COMMON_TOP/html/bin/ appsweb_$CONTEXT_NAME.cfg file are shown in Table 2-7. Key parameters in the $APPL_TOP/$CONTEXT_NAME.env file are listed in Table 2-8.

Table 2-7. *Key Parameters in the* appsweb_$CONTEXT_NAME.cfg *File*

Context File Parameter	Parameter in appsweb_$CONTEXT_NAME.cfg	Example Value	Description
s_formshost	serverName	fs1	Name of Forms Server
s_formsdomain	domainName	domain.com	Name of domain for Forms Server
s_frmConnectMode	connectMode	Socket	Mode of connecting to Forms Server (either socket or https)
s_jinit_ver_comma	jinit_ver_name	1,3,1,21	Comma delimited version of JInitiator
s_jinit_clsid	jinit_class_id	ABCDE-0013-0001-0021-ZYXWV	Class ID for JInitiator

Table 2-8. *Key Parameters in the* $CONTEXT_NAME.env *File*

Context File Parameter	Parameter in $CONTEXT_NAME.env	Example Value	Description
s_f60webcfg	FORMS60_WEB_CONFIG_FILE	appsweb_$CONTEXT_NAME.cfg	Location of Forms configuration file

Forms Metric Server and Forms Metric Client

The configuration of the Forms Metric Server and Forms Metric Client are relevant for advanced configurations of the E-Business Suite using load balancing Forms Nodes. The details for enabling this configuration beyond the scope for this guide, but some of the general configuration issues for this method of load balancing will be discussed.

Load balancing Forms in this way requires a Forms Metric Server and at least two Forms Metric Clients. The Metric Clients can be defined on separate nodes or they can be defined on the same node as the Metric Server. The first step is to identify a Web Node to be the primary Forms Metric Server. This process will balance Forms traffic across other nodes. The other Web Nodes will then need to be configured to recognize Forms traffic. MetaLink Note 217368.1 provides details on performing these tasks.

Key context file parameters for Forms Metric Servers and Clients are listed in Table 2-9.

Table 2-9. *Key Context File Parameters for Forms Metric Load Balancing*

Context File Parameter	Example Value	Description
s_formsfndtop	/vis/appltop/fnd/11.5.0	Location of Forms Server FND_TOP
s_leastloadedhost	fs1.domain.com	Set on Web Nodes to determine primary Forms Metric Server
s_meterrorurl	http://vis.domain.com/ OA_HTML/error.html	Default Metric Server error web page
s_methost	fs1.domain.com	Hostname running primary Forms Metric Server process

The other method for load balancing Forms requires that Web Nodes also be defined to support Forms Nodes. Details for enabling this method are described in MetaLink Note 201340.1. You should verify which method works best for your installation if there is a need to load balance Forms traffic.

Concurrent Processing Node Configuration

Most Concurrent Manager configuration pertains to the name and location of the output files and log files generated by the concurrent requests. The other important related topic is the Report Review Agent that is used by the application to view these output and log files. Advanced configuration related to Parallel Concurrent Processing is out of scope for this guide.

Basic Configuration

The basic configuration parameters for the Concurrent Processing Node are found in the applications environment file, and the script that starts the Concurrent Manager processes references these environment variables. (Environment files are discussed further in the "Admin Node Configuration" section of this chapter.) The key parameters in the $APPL_TOP/ $CONTEXT_NAME.env file are listed in Table 2-10.

Table 2-10. *Key Parameters in the* $CONTEXT_NAME.env *File*

Context File Parameter	Parameter in $CONTEXT_NAME.env	Example Value	Description
s_appcpnam	APPCPNAM	REQID	Determines how Concurrent Manager files are named
s_applcsf	APPLCSF	$COMMON_TOP/ $CONTEXT_NAME	Location of Concurrent Manager log and output directories
s_appllog	APPLLOG	log	Directory for log files located under $APPLCSF
s_applout	APPLOUT	out	Directory for output files located under $APPLCSF

If the Concurrent Processing Nodes are load balanced, they will need to be able to write their log and output files to a common location. As a result, the APPLCSF variable will have to be set to a location that all nodes can access.

■**Caution** Depending upon the number of concurrent requests run by your organization, the APPLCSF directory may contain a large number of files. Ensure that there is adequate space in that filesystem.

Configuring the Report Review Agent (FNDFS)

The Report Review Agent (FNDFS) is a text viewer used by Oracle applications for viewing log and output files of Concurrent Manager requests. The FNDFS executable uses the Report Review Agent Listener in the 8.0.6 Oracle Home installed on the application tier. Configuration files of interest for the Report Review Agent Listener are listener.ora and tnsnames.ora. These files are located in $ORACLE_HOME/network/admin.

The FNDFS Listener should be configured automatically by the system, but in the event of problems, it is useful to understand the FNDFS configuration and the underlying processes that run to support it.

Configuring the FNDFS Listener

When the user makes a request to view a report, the FNDFS program is launched. The following is an excerpt from the listener.ora file for the VIS instance:

```
APPS_VIS =
(ADDRESS_LIST =
    (ADDRESS= (PROTOCOL= TCP)(HOST= myappsserver)(PORT= 19005))
)
SID_LIST_APPS_VIS =
(SID_LIST =
  ( SID_DESC =
    ( SID_NAME = FNDFS  )
    ( ORACLE_HOME = /vis/oratop/8.0.6 )
    ( PROGRAM = $FND_TOP/BIN/FNDFS )
    ( NVS='EPC_DISABLED=TRUE,NLS_LANG=AMERICAN_AMERICA.US7ASCII' ))
```

Configuring FNDFS Connectivity

Within the $TNS_ADMIN/tnsname.ora file, an alias is created for FNDFS_nodename, as seen in the following excerpt from the tnsnames.ora file:

```
FNDFS_myappsserver=
(DESCRIPTION=
  (ADDRESS=(PROTOCOL=TCP)
   (HOST=myappsserver)
   (PORT=19005))
  (CONNECT_DATA=(SID=FNDFS))
)
```

The tnsnames.ora file defines connections to the FNDFS Listener, and it contains an address list of all services that you can connect to from the client.

Admin Node Configuration

In addition to the context file, there are other important configuration files located on the Admin Node, such as the application environment files, the identity.obj file, and the database connection file. We will also discuss configuring the Generic Service Management (GSM).

Application Environment Files

Oracle Applications uses several environment files to define environment variables. Environment files typically have a .env extension. The adovars.env file is located in the $APPL_TOP/admin directory. In the $APPL_TOP directory, APPLSYS.env and $CONTEXT_NAME.env are additional environment files.

Examples of environment variables defined in the environment files are FND_TOP, AD_TOP, and CLASSPATH. The CLASSPATH variable is one of the most important environment variables, and it is defined in the adovars.env file; in the context file, the variable is referenced as s_adovar_classpath. A wide variety of errors can occur if this variable is not set correctly. The value of the CLASSPATH variable is displayed in the following example:

```
$echo $CLASSPATH
```

```
CLASSPATH=$OA_JRE_TOP/lib/rt.jar:$OA_JRE_TOP/lib/i18n.jar ➡
$JAVA_TOP/appsborg.zip:$JAVA_TOP/apps.zip:  ➡
$ORACLE_HOME/forms60/java:$JAVA_TOP
```

■**Tip** Each application product has an environment variable that defines the "top" of its directory structure. For example, for Accounts Payable, the product code is AP and its "top" environment variable is $AP_TOP. All application tops are defined in the application environment files.

Administering the identity.obj File

The identity.obj file is located in the application owner's $HOME directory, and it is the identity database file that holds trusted digital certificates. If there are problems with this file, regeneration of JAR files may fail during patch applications, or a yellow warning bar may appear at the bottom of the application screens.

The identity.obj file can be re-created with the adjkey command. This command will prompt for an entity name and an organization name, as in this example:

```
$adjkey -initialize
```

Administering the Database Connection File

The database connection (DBC) file is located in the $FND_TOP/secure directory. It is used by the application to establish connections to the database. The name of the DBC file is <host>_<context_name>.dbc.

The DBC file contains connection information for the application as well as guest account details. JDeveloper also uses the DBC file for connectivity to the database. Users of JDeveloper will require a copy of the DBC file to be installed on the client workstation that is being used to develop code.

As of Oracle Application (OA) Framework version 5.10, JDBC connection pool parameters are also set in the DBC file. To tune the number of database connections created by self-service users, connection pool parameters can be modified. The key parameter settings in the DBC file are shown in Table 2-11.

Table 2-11. *Key Parameters in the DBC File*

Context File Parameter	Parameter in DBC File	Description
s_guest_user/ s_guest_pass	GUEST_USER_PWD	Guest account
s_dbhost	DB_HOST	Database hostname
s_dbport	DB_PORT	Port number for database listener
s_dbSid	DB_NAME	Database name
s_fnd_jdbc_buffermin	FND_JDBC_BUFFER_MIN	Minimum number of connections the pool maintains
s_fnd_jdbc_buffermax	FND_JDBC_BUFFER_MAX	Maximum number of connections the pool allows
s_fnd_jdbc_buffer_ decay_interval	FND_JDBC_BUFFER_ DECAY_INTERVAL	Specifies how often the connection pool checks buffer size
s_fnd_jdbc_buffer_ decay_size	FND_JDBC_BUFFER_ DECAY_SIZE	Maximum number of connections removed during a cycle

Configuring Generic Service Management

Generic Service Management (GSM) is a feature added in Oracle Applications 11*i* to manage the middle-tier services required by Oracle Applications. The services controlled by GSM include HTTP Servers, Forms Listeners, Workflow Mailer, and others. Prior to enabling GSM, these processes were manually managed by the Oracle Applications DBA.

Service Managers exist on each host in order to communicate with the Internal Concurrent Manger (ICM), which manages the required services. The ICM is also able to restart services that encounter an unexpected failure—this feature provides a greater level of availability for the applications. An easy-to-use interface to the ICM is provided by OAM, through which the Applications DBA can restart, configure, and monitor all available services.

If AD Configuration is enabled on an instance running Oracle Applications version 11.5.7 or later, then GSM is enabled by default. If GSM is not enabled, it is recommended that this be done using the application context file. Once that file has been created and the necessary GSM prerequisite patches have been applied, the $FND_TOP/patch/115/bin/cpgsmcfg.sh script can be executed to configure GSM. This script will require both the path to the application context file and the apps user password.

When configuring GSM, it may be necessary to review log files for each node's Service Manager. These log files are located in the $APPLCSF/$APPLLOG directory. The log files are named FNDSMxxxx.mgr.

■Tip Systems with a multiple-node configuration should use Parallel Concurrent Processing for GSM to take advantage of the additional nodes. In order to use this feature, you should ensure that the APPLDCP environment variable is set to ON and that a primary node has been assigned.

Errors that occur with GSM are typically a result of configuration problems with the FNDSM Listener, which is used by GSM to connect to Oracle Applications. Verify that listener.ora and tnsnames.ora have the appropriate configuration. Within the node's tnsnames.ora file, entries should be included of this form:

```
FNDSM_<node_name>_<ORACLE_SID> = (DESCRIPTION=
    (ADDRESS=(PROTOCOL=tcp)(HOST=<node_name>)(PORT=<port_number>))
    (CONNECT_DATA=(SID=FNDSM_<ORACLE_SID>))
    )
```

Additional Service Components

In addition to the configuration items already described, there are several other items that merit special consideration. These topics include TCF Socket, Discoverer Server, and Fulfillment Server.

TCF Socket

The Thin Client Framework (TCF) is a server process that uses JDBC thin drivers to manage connections for Hierarchy Editor applications such as Object Navigator. This process utilizes the TCF:HOST and TCF:PORT profile options.

Parameters in the context file pertaining to the TCF are shown in Table 2-12.

Table 2-12. *Key Control File Parameters for TCF Server*

Context File Parameter	Description
s_tcfport	Port used by TCF
s_tcfname	Name of TCF process
s_tcflog	Location of log file for TCF process
s_tcftimeout	Timeout setting for TCF process
s_tcfctrl	Location of control script for TCF process

To validate the TCF configuration, you can use the following URL:

`http://[hostname]:[port]/oa_servlets/oracle.apps.fnd.tcf.SocketServer`

This test can also be accessed from the System Administration ➤ Diagnostics ➤ TCF Status application menu.

Discoverer Server

Discoverer is a GUI tool that can be used for ad hoc queries against the Oracle Applications data. Information on using Discoverer with Oracle Applications can be found in MetaLink Note 313418.1.

When performing upgrades to Discoverer or the E-Business Suite, validate that your existing configuration remains valid. Parameters in the context file pertaining to the Discoverer Server are shown in Table 2-13.

Table 2-13. *Key Context File Parameters for Discoverer Server*

Context File Parameter	Description
s_disco_standalone	Determines whether the application is configured to use a stand-alone Discoverer Server
s_disco_machine	Location of machine running Discoverer services
s_disco_port	The port configured to listen for Discoverer requests
s_disco_ver_comma	The comma-delimited version of Discoverer
s_disco_eul_prefix	The Discoverer End User Layer (EUL) prefix

Fulfillment Server

Customer Relation Management (CRM) products, also known as the JTF product family of the E-Business Suite, include the setup of the JTF Fulfillment Server. For CRM customers, the JTF Fulfillment Server configuration is vital to the functionality of their application.

Parameters in the context file pertaining to the JTF Fulfillment Server are shown in Table 2-14.

Table 2-14. *Key Context File Parameters for JTF Server*

Context File Parameter	Description
s_jtfuf_port	Port used by JTF
s_jtftop	Location of JTF binaries
s_jtffsname	Name of JTF process
s_jtffslog	Location of log file for JTF process
s_jtffcsrvtimeout	Timeout setting for JTF process
s_jtffcsrvctrl	Location of control script for JTF process
s_jtffstart	Command to start JTF process

Database Node Configuration

The configuration of the Database Node will focus primarily on the database initialization file and files required for database connectivity. We'll also discuss the Oracle Applications Tablespace Model (OATM), as well as tips for creating custom database objects. This section assumes that you have a basic understanding of how Oracle databases function.

Database Initialization File

Database initialization parameters define the configuration settings, including memory settings, that will be used when the database is started or running.

With Oracle9*i* and prior versions, the initialization file's default location is in the $ORACLE_HOME/dbs directory on the database server. The name of the file is init[ORACLE_SID].ora; where [ORACLE_SID] is the name of the database instance. Some of the initialization parameter options may be altered dynamically; others require the database to be restarted in order to be set. With either option, the init[ORACLE_SID].ora file must be updated if the change is to remain after the next bounce of the instance.

Beginning with version Oracle9*i*, the database initialization file may be replaced with an spfile, and with Oracle Database 10*g* (Oracle10*g*), the spfile is mandatory. The spfile is a binary file stored on the database server. It is intended to improve the management of the database instance by eliminating the need to manually edit the init[ORACLE_SID].ora text file.

It is possible to convert the Oracle9*i* database to use an `spfile` by using a simple SQL statement:

```
SQL> create spfile from pfile =
'/u01/oracle/product/dbs/initVIS.ora';
```

When using an `spfile`, initialization parameters can be modified with `alter system` statements while you are connected to the database. Here's an example:

```
SQL> alter system set processes =2000 scope=spfile;
```

■**Tip** Initialization parameters are sometimes deprecated with new versions of the database. Be sure to review new and deprecated initialization parameters when upgrading to a new version of the database.

Oracle provides some recommended and mandatory settings for the database initialization parameters of the E-Business Suite. Refer to MetaLink Note 216205.1 for a detailed listing. It is important to match the recommended settings where possible; however, due to environment-specific naming conventions or bugs, this is not always possible. A list of common Oracle9*i* and Oracle10*g* database initialization parameters for Oracle Applications 11.5.10 are shown in Table 2-15.

Table 2-15. *Common Oracle Applications 11i Database Initialization Parameters for Oracle9*i *and Oracle10*g

Initialization Parameter	Recommended Value	Description
db_name	*Environment dependent*	Name of the database. This value is environment dependent.
control_files	*Environment dependent*	Location and name of database controlfiles. It is preferable to create three controlfiles on different disk volumes in case of a hardware failure. This value is environment dependent.
db_block_size	8192	Database block size. For Oracle Applications this must be set to 8192.

Continued

Table 2-15. *Continued*

Initialization Parameter	Recommended Value	Description
Compatible	*Version dependent*	The version of the database. For example, 9.2.0 or 10.1.0.
_system_trig_enabled	TRUE	Enables system triggers.
07_dictionary_accessibility	*Version dependent*	This parameter enables data dictionary querying. For Oracle Applications 11.5.10 it can be set to FALSE. For versions 11.5.9 and lower, this parameter must be set to TRUE.
nls_date_format	DD-MON-RR	Default date format.
nls_sort	BINARY	When set to BINARY, the collating sequence for the ORDER BY clause is based on the numeric values of characters.
nls_comp	BINARY	When set to BINARY, comparisons in the WHERE clause and in PL/SQL blocks are binary.
nls_length_semantics	BYTE	Required for NLS and character sets.
max_enabled_roles	100	Some applications require max_enabled_roles to be set. This must be set to 100 for Oracle Applications.
background_dump_dest	*Environment dependent*	Destination for background dump files.
core_dump_dest	*Environment dependent*	Destination for core dump files.
user_dump_dest	*Environment dependent*	Destination for user trace and dump files.
cursor_sharing	EXACT	Determines which types of SQL statements can share cursors. It must be set to EXACT for Oracle Applications.
aq_tm_processes	1	Enables time monitoring of queue messages.
job_queue_processes	2	Maximum number of processes created for execution of jobs.

Initialization Parameter	Recommended Value	Description
Log_archive_start	TRUE	Enables automatic archive logging.
db_file_multiblock_read_count	8	Maximum number of blocks read during an I/O scan.
optimizer_max_permutations	200	Maximum number of table permutations considered for optimizing joins in order to reduce parse time.
query_rewrite_enabled	TRUE	Enables query rewriting.
_sort_elimination_cost_ratio	5	Affects cost based optimizer.
_like_with_bind_as_equality	TRUE	Affects cost based optimizer.
_fast_full_scan_enabled	FALSE	Affects cost based optimizer.
_sqlexec_progression_cost	2147483647	Affects cost based optimizer.
undo_management	AUTO	Enables system managed undo.
undo_tablespace	*Environment dependent*	Name of the undo tablespace.
pga_aggregate	1G	Auto memory manager is used as of Oracle9*i*, which replaces sort_area_size and hash_area_size. The initial value of 1G may need to be adjusted.
Workarea_size_policy	AUTO	Allows system to automatically size PGA based upon pga_aggregate_target.
olap_page_pool_size	4193404	Specifies the size (in bytes) of the OLAP pool.

■**Tip** For the dump destination parameters, set up a common filesystem such as /oracle/admin/$DBNAME to place these log files in. This will ease management and monitoring of these files. For example, background_dump_dest=/oracle/admin/ VIS/bdump.

Oracle9*i* database initialization parameters for Oracle Applications 11.5.10 are shown in Table 2-16, and those for Oracle10*g* are in Table 2-17.

Table 2-16. *Oracle9i Database Initialization Parameters for 11.5.10*

Initialization Parameter	Recommended Value	Description
optimizer_features_enable	9.2.0	Controls the behavior of Oracle's optimizer.
undo_retention	1800	Length of time in seconds the system preserves undo information.
undo_suppress_errors	FALSE	Suppresses ORA-30019 errors from setting rollback segments.
_index_join_enabled	FALSE	Affects cost based optimizer.
_b_tree_bitmap_plans	FALSE	Affects cost based optimizer.
db_cache_size	156M	Specifies the size of the buffer cache. 156M is the minimum requirement for 11*i* applications; this parameter will need to be adjusted depending upon application usage.
java_pool_size	50M	Memory allocated for Java Virtual Machine. An initial size of 50M is recommended, but this may need to be adjusted.
log_buffer	10485760	Size for buffering entries in redo log file. The value is dependent upon application usage.
shared_pool_size	300M	Memory allocated for data dictionary and SQL statements. The value is dependent upon application usage. An initial size of 300M is recommended, but this value may need to be adjusted.
shared_pool_size_reserved	30M	Allocation of shared pool for large objects.
_shared_pool_reserved_min_alloc	4100	Allocation of reserved memory for the shared pool.

Table 2-17. *Oracle10g Database Initialization Parameters for 11.5.10*

Initialization Parameter	Recommended Value	Description
plsql_optimizer_level	2	Enables PL/SQL global optimizer and native compilation.
plsql_code_type	NATIVE	Enables PL/SQL global optimizer and native compilation.
_b_tree_bitmap_plans	FALSE	Required for the cost based optimizer for 11*i* applications.
sga_target	570M	For Oracle10g, SGA memory is set with the automatic SGA tuning parameter. Entering the total size of the SGA allows the system to tune the caches. The value of 570M is the minimum recommendation and may need to be adjusted.

■**Tip** With Oracle10g, the use of automatic SGA tuning, enabled with the sga_target parameter, replaces many of the memory parameters previously defined, including db_cache_size, large_pool_size, log_buffer, shared_pool_size, and java_pool_size.

Reviewing Database Initialization Parameters

You can query the v$parameter view in order to get a listing of all the current initialization settings. The results can be spooled to a file that can be stored for later reference:

```
SQL> spool db_parameters.log
SQL> select name, value
SQL> from v$parameter order by name;
SQL> spool off
```

To retrieve the value for one setting, the show parameter [name or partial parameter name] command can be used within SQL*Plus. This is the fastest way to check a small number of values:

```
SQL> show parameter processes
```

NAME	TYPE	VALUE
aq_tm_processes	integer	5
db_writer_processes	integer	1
job_queue_processes	integer	10
log_archive_max_processes	integer	2
processes	integer	1000

Rather than manually checking all initialization settings, Oracle provides a script called bde_chk_cbo.sql to help verify the values. Details regarding the bde_chk_cbo.sql script can be found in MetaLink Note 174605.1. When this script is executed, a report containing the database initialization parameters will be generated. You may review this report in order to validate recommended database initialization settings.

▪**Tip** Some initialization settings, particularly those related to system memory, such as db_cache_size and pga_aggregate_target, will be dependent upon application usage. Resolution of application issues and SRs may also require non-recommended database initialization parameters. Be sure to document reasons parameters differ from the recommended settings.

Database Network Configuration

In order to establish remote connections to the database instance, the database listener must be properly configured. The files related to this configuration are the listener.ora and tnsnames.ora files, which are located in the $TNS_ADMIN directory. These files describe the port number, instance name, and server that remote connections use to access the instance. There are also timeout settings and trace level settings that may need to be adjusted.

Configuring the Database Listener

The database listener defines the protocol, server, port, and database for which the database listener is able to service connection requests. The following is an excerpt from the listener.ora file:

```
VIS=
  (ADDRESS_LIST =
   (ADDRESS= (PROTOCOL=IPC)(KEY=VIS))
   (ADDRESS=(PROTOCOL=TCP)
     (Host=mydbserver)
     (Port=19000))
  )
CONNECT_TIMEOUT_VIS=0
TRACE_LEVEL_VIS=OFF
```

When the database configuration files have been created, the database listener can be started and stopped with the lsnrctl database utility. This utility can be run with a start, stop, or status parameter.

Configuring the Remote Database Connection

Remote database connections are managed by configuring the tnsnames.ora file on the client. This file contains an address list of all databases that you need to connect to from the client. The address list includes the protocol, server, port, and database that will be connected to when referencing the service name. The following is an excerpt from the tnsnames.ora file for connecting to the VIS service name:

```
VIS=
(DESCRIPTION=
  (ADDRESS=(PROTOCOL=TCP)
    (HOST=mydbserver)
    (PORT=19000))
  (CONNECT_DATA=(SID=VIS))
)
```

Validating Database Network Configuration

To validate database network configuration, the tnsping command can be used. Here's an example of its use:

```
$tnsping vis
```

```
TNS Ping Utility: Version 9.2.0.6.0 - Vision on
25-JUL-2005 16:36:22

Copyright (c) 1997 Oracle Corporation. All rights reserved.

Used parameter files:

Used TNSNAMES adapter to resolve the alias
Attempting to contact (DESCRIPTION=
(ADDRESS=(PROTOCOL=tcp)(HOST=mydbserver)(PORT=19000))
(CONNECT_DATA=(SID=VIS)))
OK (290 msec)
```

Oracle Applications Tablespace Model

To simplify the management of the Oracle Applications Database, Oracle has introduced the Oracle Applications Tablespace Model (OATM). This model helps to reduce management overhead by limiting the number of tablespaces used by the application. The OATM requires a database version of 9.2.0.4 or later. Additional details regarding OATM may be found in MetaLink Note 248857.1.

With older versions of the E-Business Suite, each product would have a data tablespace and an index tablespace, so the number of tablespaces required by the system increases two-fold with the number of enabled products. This can result in several hundred tablespaces and corresponding datafiles. If the maximum number of datafiles is set too low in the database, problems can occur due to this growth.

With OATM, Oracle has reduced the number of tablespaces required for the application to twelve. By limiting the number of tablespaces, there should be less wasted storage space due to overhead from tablespaces containing little data. This approach also allows for a smaller number of datafiles. The standard tablespaces used with OATM are shown in Table 2-18.

Table 2-18. *OATM Tablespaces*

Tablespace Name	Description
APPS_TS_TX_DATA	Contains transactional data
APPS_TS_TX_IDX	Contains indexes for transactional tables
APPS_TS_SEED	Contains reference and setup data and indexes
APPS_TS_INTERFACE	Contains interface and temporary data and indexes
APPS_TS_SUMMARY	Contains summary objects, such as materialized views
APPS_TS_NOLOGGING	Contains materialized views not used for summary management
APPS_TS_QUEUES	Contains Advanced Queuing dependent tables and indexes
APPS_TS_MEDIA	Contains multimedia objects, such as video, sound, and spatial data
APPS_TS_ARCHIVE	Contains purge-related objects
UNDO	The Automatic Undo Management tablespace
TEMP	The temporary tablespace, used for sorting and temporary tables
SYSTEM	The system tablespace

The APPS_TS_MEDIA tablespace can become very large, especially if your organization is using a lot of LOB data. If that is the case, be sure to use the techniques described in Chapters 3 and 6 to monitor tablespace and file-system growth.

Creating Custom Database Objects

At times it may be necessary to create custom database objects, such as tables or indexes, in the Oracle E-Business Suite database. If this is required, it is recommended that a custom schema be created as the owner of the database customizations. The custom schema should also have its own data and index tablespaces.

Creating a custom schema in this manner will isolate all customizations from the packaged application and provide ease of support and manageability for both the custom objects and standard Oracle application objects.

Additional Configuration Topics

In addition to node-level configuration, there are other miscellaneous configuration options and topics that are part of managing the E-Business Suite. This section will provide an overview of the following additional configuration topics:

- Using the configuration wizards from OAM
- Using OAM to review licensed products and license new products
- Configuring password security at the application and database level

There are also some important parameters in the application context file and some additional system files to be covered briefly.

Configuration Wizards

Several advanced configurations can be enabled using wizards from the OAM utility. Navigate to the Site Map menu and select Administration ➤ AutoConfig ➤ Configuration Wizards to display these options. Figure 2-3 shows the configuration wizard options available.

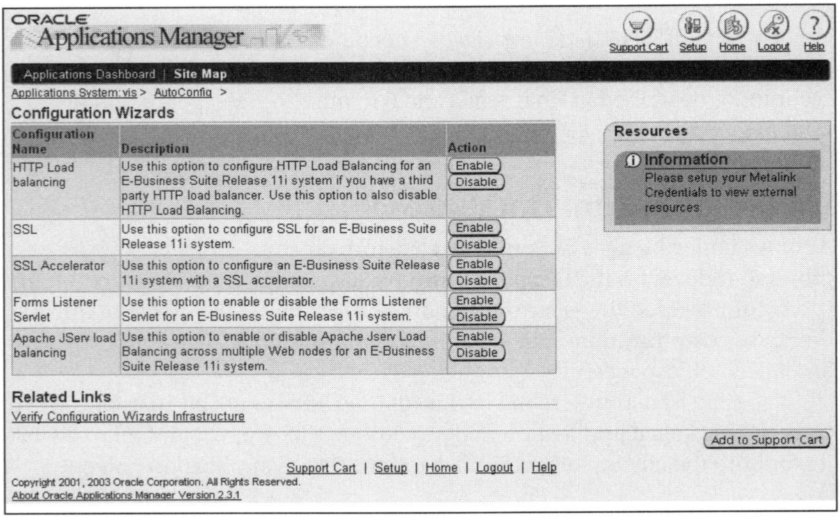

Figure 2-3. *OAM configuration wizards*

License Manager

It is sometimes necessary to review licensed products or license new products for the Oracle E-Business Suite. These functions can be easily achieved using OAM's interface to the Oracle License Manager.

Reviewing Licensed Products

To review the currently licensed products in the application, OAM provides a user-friendly searchable interface, as shown in Figure 2-4. To access this feature after logging into OAM, select Site Map ➤ License Manager ➤ License ➤ Products.

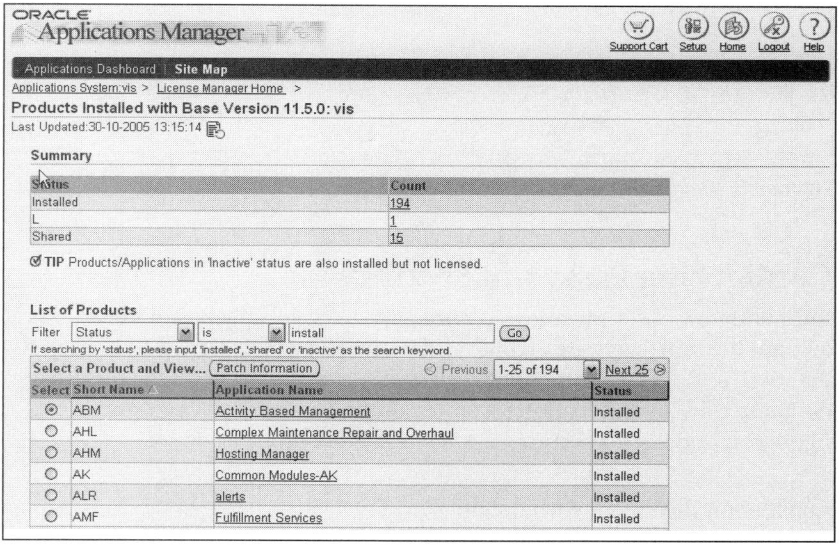

Figure 2-4. *Viewing licensed products in OAM*

Licensing Additional Products

OAM also provides a user-friendly interface for licensing additional products in the application. To access this feature after logging into OAM, select Site Map ➤ License Manager ➤ License ➤ Products. On this screen, shown in Figure 2-5, select the product to license by clicking on the box beside it, and then click Next. The product is then licensed.

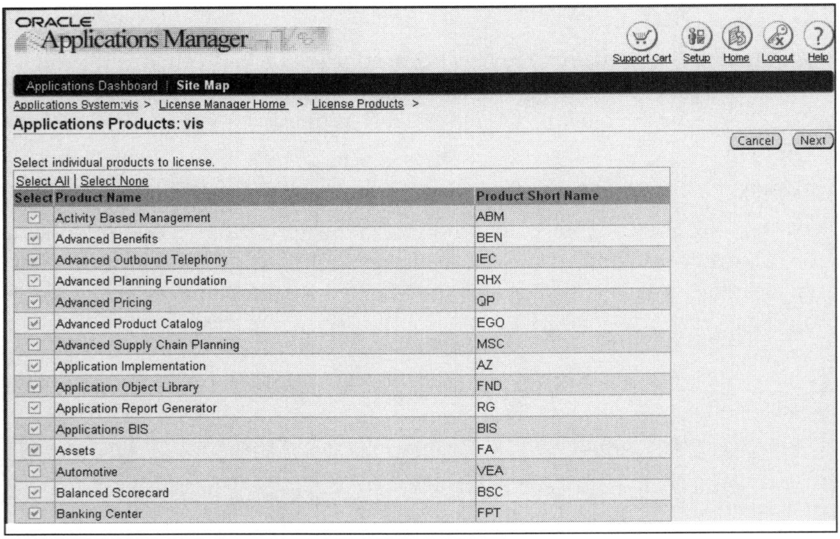

Figure 2-5. *Viewing products that can be licensed in OAM*

Configuring Password Security

Improving Oracle Applications security can be accomplished at the database and application levels. Password validation can be maintained by both the database and application. Additionally, users can be limited to access via database roles or application responsibilities. This section will provide configuration options for securing application and database logins.

Application Password Verification

At the application level, profile settings can be used to add security to the application user passwords. These profile options assist in providing passwords that follow defined standards. Table 2-19 outlines the profile options used to provide password security for application users.

Table 2-19. *Profile Options Available for Application Password Security*

Profile Option	Description
Signon Password Hard to Guess	When set to YES, the password must contain at least one letter or number. It may not contain the username, and it cannot contain repeating characters.
Signon Password Length	When set to a nonnegative integer, the password will be required to be the specific length.

Profile Option	Description
Signon Password Failure Limit	When set to a nonnegative integer, the user will not be able to log in again after the number of unsuccessful logins equal to the set value.
Signon Password No Reuse	When set to a nonnegative integer, the user will not be able to reuse his or her password for the number of days equal to the set value.
Signon Password Custom	You may create your own custom validation Java class for password verification. The details are outside the scope of this guide, but the option is available for your use.

Database Password Verification

The Applications DBA can define additional password security for users defined in the database. This may be accomplished through password verification functions and database profiles. Password verification functions, once defined, may be assigned to the database profile, which is then assigned to the database user.

The database profile feature has several standard options, such as the ability to lock the account after a set number of failed login attempts. Additionally, the profile allows for the creation of a customized password verification function to enforce password complexity. Password verification functions define specific requirements for the content of a password, including length, characters, and special characters, to name a few. The following is an example password function that checks all passwords for a special character, such as "#" or "_":

```
CREATE OR REPLACE FUNCTION "SYS"."PASSWORD_VERIFY_FUNCTION" (
username varchar2,
password varchar2,
old_password varchar2)
RETURN boolean IS
n boolean;
m integer;
isspecial boolean;
specialarray varchar2(25);

BEGIN
specialarray:='#_';
```

```
-- Check for required special character
isspecial:=FALSE;
FOR i IN 1..length(specialarray) LOOP
FOR j IN 1..m LOOP
IF substr(password,j,1) = substr(specialarray,i,1) THEN
isspecial:=TRUE;
END IF;
END LOOP;
END LOOP;
IF isspecial = FALSE THEN
raise_application_error(-20001, 'The password should contain one of
the following special characters # or _ ');
END IF;

-- Everything is fine, return TRUE ;
RETURN(TRUE);
END;
```

Miscellaneous Configuration

This section will cover a few important miscellaneous configuration parameters in the application context file, and in the oraInst.loc and oratab files, that have not been previously covered.

█Note On UNIX, oraInst.loc and oratab are two additional configuration files of interest. The Oracle Universal Installer (OUI) and the AD Clone utility use these files. These files are located in either the /etc or /var/opt directory, depending upon your flavor of UNIX.

Miscellaneous Parameters in the Application Context File

There are hundreds of parameters in the application context file. Some commonly used context file entries that were not previously covered in this chapter are shown in Table 2-20.

Table 2-20. *Additional Miscellaneous Context File Parameters*

Context File Parameter	Description
s_contextname	Context name used by system
s_dbSid	Database SID name
s_jinit_ver_dot	Version information for JInitiator
s_jdk_top	Home directory for Java Development Kit
s_adperlprg	Location of Perl program

Managing the oraInst.loc File

If performing any maintenance to the Oracle install, the oraInst.loc file needs to be set to the target install ORACLE_HOME on the server where the maintenance is being performed. The Oracle Universal Installer and AD Clone use the oraInst.loc file to determine Oracle install location.

Here is an example of the contents of oraInst.loc:

```
inventory_loc=/vis/oratop/iAS
group=dba
```

■**Tip** If multiple instances are running on the same physical server, ensure that the oraInst.loc file has the correct instance information before performing maintenance.

Managing the oratab File

The /etc/oratab file should have only one entry for each database on the database server and one entry for each ORACLE_HOME for the application nodes. The oratab file is also used by the Oracle Intelligent Agent and standard Oracle shutdown and startup scripts (dbshut and dbstart).

This is an example of the contents of the oratab on the database server:

```
#ORACLE_SID:ORACLE_HOME:Y/N
VIS:/vis/oratop/10.2.0.1:Y
```

An example of the contents of the oratab file on the application server is as follows:

```
#ORACLE_SID:ORACLE_HOME:Y/N
*:/vis/oratop/iAS
```

▓**Tip** After performing clones or upgrades, the oratab file may become cluttered with additional entries. You should periodically clean up the oratab file to remove extra or unused entries.

Configuration Best Practices

When making modifications to configuration files, you should create a change log to document your changes. Manually documenting changes will provide a means of review, and it is an important part of managing the application. When applying patches, or upgrading any components of the application, you should be aware of and document any possible changes to configuration settings. If configuration changes involve memory- or performance-related settings, stress test the change in a test environment before promoting the change to production.

If a test or development instance is used to simulate production loads or tests, then we recommend that the instance be sized to match settings in the production instance; otherwise, reducing sizing parameters can save CPU and memory resources on test or development servers. For example, limiting memory resources on the database server can be achieved by reducing the database memory initialization parameters, such as db_cache_size and pga_aggregate for Oracle9*i*, and sga_size for Oracle10*g*. Reducing minspareservers and maxspareservers for the Apache server may also reduce resource consumption for the applications tier. These are only a few examples of parameters that can be modified to reduce CPU and memory resource requirements for test and development servers.

CHAPTER 3

■ ■ ■

Monitoring and Troubleshooting

Typical day-to-day tasks of an Oracle Applications DBA involve monitoring and troubleshooting the Oracle E-Business Suite. Through proactive monitoring of the application, many troubleshooting requirements and potential performance issues can be identified or eliminated. Due to the overwhelming benefit of such monitoring, the Applications DBA should spend a significant amount of time developing an extensive proactive monitoring process.

This chapter will cover a variety of monitoring and troubleshooting topics and techniques:

- **Methods for monitoring**: Proactive monitoring of Oracle Applications can alert you to problems before they happen. We'll look at monitoring scripts, options for scheduling scripts with `crontab`, and using monitoring tools such as Enterprise Manager 10*g* Grid Control.

- **Database monitoring**: Monitoring critical aspects of the database can assist you in keeping the system running properly. This section will detail specific monitoring and troubleshooting techniques for the database, including monitoring log files, database availability, session information, and storage usage.

- **Apache monitoring**: Keeping your Web Node running efficiently is important for providing a positive user experience in your environment. Apache monitoring includes reviewing log files, checking Apache availability, validating its configuration, and monitoring the JVM pool. OAM options for Apache and JServ monitoring will also be described.

- **Forms monitoring**: This section will look at how to review Forms sessions by using OAM and monitoring for dump files.

- **Concurrent Manager monitoring**: Concurrent Manager issues can cause problems with scheduled requests, so it is important to gauge its well-being. This section will include an outline of how to monitor Concurrent Manager log and output files and the running and pending concurrent requests. It will also include details for canceling an active concurrent request. Monitoring Concurrent Manager requests with OAM will also be covered.

- **Server monitoring**: Often issues surface first on the server; as such, measuring usage on the server is one of the best methods of proactive monitoring. This section will explain details for monitoring server availability, CPU usage, and filesystem free space.

- **Network monitoring**: Networking related problems can be quite troublesome to pinpoint for an Applications DBA. In this section, we'll look at using the `ping` and `tracert` commands, plus cover the use of the Network Test provided within the application to assist with troubleshooting networking issues.

- **Additional monitoring and troubleshooting**: There are some additional items that should be examined as well. Additional monitoring for application profile changes and system backups will be covered in this section.

Finally, we'll look briefly at best practices for monitoring and troubleshooting. These tools should help you resolve errors that occur more quickly and prevent many errors from occurring at all.

■**Tip** The steps involved in monitoring the application will differ depending upon usage and current release levels of technology stack components. During a major upgrade or product rollout, the Applications DBA should spend time looking for new monitoring requirements and also verify that existing monitoring tasks are still sufficient.

Methods for Monitoring

Throughout this chapter, scripts will be provided to assist you with day-to-day monitoring tasks. These scripts can be used with monitoring tools such as Enterprise Manager (EM) 10g Grid Control or other third-party monitoring tools to enhance and provide additional user-defined monitoring capabilities. However, you may find that many of these monitoring tasks are already performed by third-party products.

If you do not have a monitoring tool such as EM 10*g* Grid Control configured for your systems, the UNIX scheduler program crontab can be used to schedule the scripts included in this chapter. Additional details regarding crontab are provided in Chapter 6 of this guide.

The scripts in this chapter include the basic SQL and UNIX commands to monitor for specific events in the database or on the server. The supplied scripts are not meant to be the final word in monitoring, but rather a starting point for you to create a proactively monitored environment. They can be modified and customized to meet your requirements and to include error handling.

The content provided for the sample scripts should be saved to a script file. It is recommended that you create a directory on each node to contain such scripts. You can then execute the script file by calling it from a UNIX prompt, scheduling it in the crontab, or executing it with a monitoring tool as a user-defined job.

Each monitoring script is set up to return a code indicating that the condition has failed or succeeded. The monitoring scripts in this chapter are modeled on three templates, shown in Listings 3-1 through 3-3. The parameters for these scripts are described in Table 3-1.

Listing 3-1. *Example of a Monitoring Script Using Template One*

```
#Comments
[THRESHOLD | LISTENER | SERVER_NAME | FORMS_DIR]=$1
[FILESYSTEM]=$2
TMPFILE=/[path]/[tempfile_name]
LOGFILE=/[path]/[logfile_name]_$ORACLE_SID.txt
unix_command > $TMPFILE
RETURN_CODE=`grep "[condition]" /[path]/[tmpfile]| wc -l`
if [ $RETURN_CODE -eq 0 ]
  then
 exit 0
else
 echo "$ORACLE_SID - [Message]" > $LOGFILE
 exit 1
fi
```

Listing 3-2. *Example of a Monitoring Script Using Template Two*

```
#Comments
[THRESHOLD]=$1
LOGFILE=/[path]/[logfile_name]_$ORACLE_SID.txt
sqlplus -s [APPS User]/[APPS Password] << EOF
  [SQL_Condition];
  exit
EOF
if [ $? -eq 0 ]
  then
    exit 0
  else
    echo "$ORACLE_SID - [Message]"> $LOGFILE
    exit 1
fi
```

Listing 3-3. *Example of a Monitoring Script Using Template Three*

```
#Comments
[THRESHOLD=$1]
LOGFILE=/[path]/[logfile_name]_$ORACLE_SID.txt
sqlplus -s [APPS User]/[APPS Password] << EOF
  spool $LOGFILE
  [SQL_Condition];
  exit
EOF
RETURN_CODE=`grep "[condition]" $LOGFILE wc -l`
if [ $RETURN_CODE -eq 0 ]
  then
    exit 0
else
  echo "$ORACLE_SID - [Message]" > $LOGFILE
  exit 1
fi
```

■**Note** For UNIX scripts, parameters passed to the script can be referenced within the script as $1, $2, etc.

Table 3-1. *Parameter Descriptions for the Monitoring Scripts in Listings 3-1 Through 3-3*

Parameter	Description	Parameter Usage
#Comments	The # character denotes comments in the script. While not mandatory, it is always beneficial to insert comments into scripts for the purpose of documentation.	Optional—it assists with script maintenance
THRESHOLD	Used to define thresholds for conditions that are being monitored. When calling the script, the value for this parameter is specified.	Optional—it depends on the event being monitored
LISTENER	Used to define the name of the listener being monitored. When calling the script, the value for this parameter is specified.	Optional—it depends on the event being monitored
SERVER_NAME	Used to define the name of the server being monitored. When calling the script, the value for this parameter is specified.	Optional—it depends on the event being monitored
FORMS_DIR	Used to define the directory from which the Forms Server is started. When calling the script, the value for this parameter is specified.	Optional—it depends on the event being monitored
FILESYSTEM	Used in the script to store the parameter for filesystems that are being monitored. When calling the script, the value for this parameter is specified.	Optional—it is only used in specific monitoring scripts
TMPFILE	Used in the script to store temporary information required for triggering a condition.	Optional—it is only used in specific monitoring scripts
LOGFILE	Used in the script to store the message that can be sent to an email address in order to alert the Applications DBA about the triggered event.	Mandatory
[APPS User]	Specifies the APPS User account; typically APPS.	Mandatory
[APPS Password]	Specifies the password for the APPS User.	Mandatory
[path]	Specifies the path where the log file is written.	Mandatory

Continued

Table 3-1. *Continued*

Parameter	Description	Parameter Usage
[logfile_name]	Specifies the name of the file that is used to store a message that can be emailed to alert an Applications DBA about the event that has been triggered.	Mandatory—it should be as descriptive as possible
[SQL_Condition]	Specifies a SQL statement used to query the database for the monitored condition.	Conditional—it is only required when results are retrieved from the database
[condition]	Specifies a condition that is retrieved with the grep command from the information captured in a log file.	Conditional—it is required when a condition is monitored on the server or in a log file
RETURN_CODE	Used to store a 0 or 1; 0 means that the condition is not met, 1 means that the condition is met.	Conditional—it is required when a condition is monitored on the server or in a log file
$ORACLE_SID	Used in order to provide detailed information about the Oracle instance that has triggered the event. It is written as part of the LOGFILE name and as content in the LOGFILE.	Mandatory
[Message]	Specifies the message that is written to the LOGFILE in order to provide details to the Applications DBA regarding the event that has been triggered.	Mandatory—it should be as descriptive as possible
Exit	The exit code for the condition being monitored. If 0, the condition is not met; if 1, the condition is met and the event is triggered.	Mandatory

▨**Note** After a UNIX command is executed, the return code can be checked using $?. A return code of 0 indicates the command completed without error.

Database Monitoring and Troubleshooting

An Applications DBA needs to be aware of the database activity in the system—over time, trends begin to develop in the database that enable the DBA to proactively monitor the database. This section will assist you in identifying and monitoring common database trends and events.

Within the database, there are several monitoring categories that require attention:

- Database alert log file and database listener log file
- Database availability
- Database sessions (idle sessions, high active sessions, high CPU consumers, total sessions, long running sessions, and blocking sessions)
- Database storage (datafile sizing, objects that are unable to extend, and maximum extent issues)

Database Log Files

When monitoring the database, it is important to review the associated database log files, particularly the database alert log file and the database listener log file.

Database Alert Log

One of the most important tasks for a database administrator is monitoring the database alert log file, located in the directory specified by the bdump database initialization parameter. All database internal errors will be logged in the database alert*.log file, and they are written in the following format: ORA-XXXXX. The Applications DBA needs to be alerted when such errors occur.

The following script can be used to monitor for errors written to the alert log:

```
#Script used to monitor the database alert log file
LOGFILE=/tmp/database_alert_$ORACLE_SID.log
RETURN_CODE=`grep ORA- /[bdump]/alert.log | wc -l`
if [ $RETURN_CODE -eq 0 ]
  then
  exit 0
else
  echo "$ORACLE_SID - There are $RETURN_CODE errors in Alert log" >
$LOGFILE
  exit 1
fi
```

■**Tip** This script may be customized to monitor for specific ORA-XXXXX errors in order to send more meaningful messages to the Applications DBA. Additionally, you may want to customize this script to ignore some of the ORA-XXXXX error messages that are posted in the alert*.log file.

In order to resolve errors that are logged in the alert log, you will need to research specifics about the errors on MetaLink. It may also be essential to open an SR in order to resolve the error. See Chapter 7 for more information on MetaLink searches and SR management.

■**Tip** Depending upon the error written in the alert log, a trace file may be written to the directory specified by the udump database initialization parameter. The trace file will contain additional details regarding the encountered error condition and will assist in resolving the issue at hand. If an SR is opened with Oracle Support, the trace file in the udump directory should be uploaded to support.

Database Listener Log

If errors are experienced with the database listener, you should review the contents of the listener log file. This log file is located in the directory and files specified by the following parameters in the $TNS_ADMIN/listener.ora configuration file, where [LISTENER] is the name of the listener:

```
LOG_FILE_[LISTENER] = [log file name]
LOG_DIRECTORY_[LISTENER] = [path to directory]
```

If necessary, additional tracing parameters may be configured for the listener to assist with troubleshooting. The following parameters control tracing levels in the listener.ora file, where [LISTENER] is the name of the listener:

```
TRACE_LEVEL_[LISTENER] = [OFF | USER | ADMIN | SUPPORT]
TRACE_FILE_[LISTENER] = [trace file name]
TRACE_DIRECTORY_[LISTENER] = [path to directory]
TRACE_TIMESTAMP_[LISTENER] = [ON or TRUE | OFF or FALSE]
```

■**Tip** For most Oracle networking issues, it is sufficient to set the
TRACE_LEVEL_LISTENER to ADMIN; you should only set the listener trace level to
SUPPORT at the request of Oracle Support.

In order to resolve errors that are logged in the database listener log, you
will need to research specifics about the errors on MetaLink. You may also be
required to open an SR in order to resolve the error.

Database Availability

The most basic monitoring for the database checks whether the database
and database listener are available. This section will focus on how the Oracle
Applications DBA can monitor database availability.

Database Up or Down

Monitoring for database availability will allow the Applications DBA to
respond as quickly as possible to a major outage. This will assist in minimizing unplanned downtime for the system.

A simple query executed on the server where the database resides can
be used to test database availability. An example script that can be used for
monitoring database availability is as follows:

```
#Script used to monitor database availability
LOGFILE=/tmp/database_down_$ORACLE_SID.txt
sqlplus -s apps/apps << EOF
  select user
  from dual;
  exit
EOF
if [ $? -eq 0 ]
  then
    exit 0
  else
    echo "$ORACLE_SID is unavailable"> $LOGFILE
    exit 1
fi
```

■**Tip** Be certain to disable database availability monitoring as well as other monitoring
scripts during periods of system maintenance.

If the database is unexpectedly unavailable, the first place to look for the source of the outage is the database alert log file. (Monitoring the `alert*.log` was discussed in the "Database Alert Log" section earlier in this chapter.) If the underlying `ORA-XXXXX` error message in the alert log is unknown, research the error on MetaLink. You may need to open an SR with Oracle Support for additional assistance.

Database Listener Up or Down

If the database listener goes down, users will be unable to establish a connection to the database. This can be tested for by using the `status` parameter of the listener control command, `lsnrctl`. Here's an example script:

```
#Script used to monitor the listener availability
LISTENER=$1
LOGFILE=/tmp/listener_$ORACLE_SID.log
lsnrctl status $LISTENER
if [ $? -eq 0 ]
  then
    exit 0
else
    echo "$LISTENER is down" > $LOGFILE
    exit 1
fi
```

If the database listener is unexpectedly unavailable, the first place to look for the source of the outage is the database listener log file. (Monitoring the listener log file was discussed in the "Database Listener Log" section earlier in the chapter.)

Session Monitoring

Monitoring database sessions is critical for ensuring that potential problems are caught before they impact the entire system. This section will cover common issues that can be identified by monitoring database sessions.

Identifying Long Idle Sessions

Sometimes users may establish a connection to the database and don't properly disconnect. Many organizations consider this to be a security risk. With a script, you can retrieve session information from the database to determine whether this is happening, and it is useful to gather as much information as possible about the session in question.

The time threshold in the monitoring script should be customized based on the requirements of your organization. Also, situations may occur where certain programs are allowed to have long idle times. For example, if connection pooling is being used for the application server, then JDBC thin client sessions may have large idle times.

The following example script will assist in monitoring sessions that have been idle for a user-determined amount of time:

```
#Script used to monitor sessions with a long idle time
#THRESHOLD is the maximum duration that an inactive session
#may remain connected to the database
THRESHOLD=$1
LOGFILE=/tmp/high_idle_$ORACLE_SID.log
sqlplus -s apps/apps << EOF
  set heading off
  spool $LOGFILE
  select distinct '$ORACLE_SID - High Idle sessions above Threshold.'
  from v\$session db_session,
    v\$process process,
    v\$session_wait wait
  where process.addr = db_session.paddr
    and db_session.sid = wait.sid
    and type='USER'
    and db_session.username is not null
    and db_session.program not like 'JDBC%'
    and last_call_et>$THRESHOLD;
  -- add data to logfile
  select db_session.username,
    db_session.osuser,
    db_session.terminal,
    db_session.sid,
    db_session.serial#,
    process.spid,
    db_session.process,
    wait.event,
    db_session.program,
    to_char(logon_time,'dd-mm-yy hh:mi am') "LOGON",
    floor(last_call_et/3600)||':'||
    floor(mod(last_call_et,3600)/60)||':'||
    mod(mod(last_call_et,3600),60) "IDLE"
  from v\$session db_session,
    v\$process process,
    v\$session_wait wait
  where process.addr = db_session.paddr
    and db_session.sid = wait.sid
    and type='USER'
```

```
  and db_session.username is not null
  and db_session.program not like 'JDBC%'
  and last_call_et>$THRESHOLD
 order by last_call_et;
 spool off
 exit
EOF
RETURN_CODE=`grep "Threshold" $LOGFILE | wc -l`
if [ $RETURN_CODE -eq 0 ]
 then
 exit 0
else
 exit 1
fi
```

Once sessions that have been idle for a long period of time are identified, you should contact the user of the session and determine whether the
process should still be executing. If it should not be running, the session
should be killed. Information on killing database and operating system
sessions is provided in Chapter 6 of this guide.

▨Tip One method for resolving this problem is prevention—you can configure all database accounts to expire after a specified amount of idle time. This option should only be
used for accounts that are not used to run the application code.

Identifying High Active Sessions

The first step in determining an expected number of active sessions for the
system is to monitor the day-to-day activity in the database for a period of
time. This will allow you to determine the number of active sessions that are
expected for your environment.

The following query will return the number of sessions in an active state:

```
SQL>select count(1) from v$session where status='ACTIVE';
```

▨Note Trending analysis for metrics that are collected is a feature of EM 10*g* Grid
Control Diagnostics Pack.

Once trending data is captured and analyzed, the following code can be used to alert the Applications DBA if the number of active sessions exceeds the predetermined threshold, creating an environment of high active sessions:

```
#Script used to monitor high active sessions
#THRESHOLD is the maximum number of high active sessions
#connected to the database at one time
THRESHOLD=$1
LOGFILE=/tmp/high_active_$ORACLE_SID.txt
sqlplus -s apps/apps << EOF
  set heading off
  spool $LOGFILE
  select '$ORACLE_SID - High Active Sessions exceeds Threshold -
' ||count(1)
  from v\$session
  where status='ACTIVE'
  having count(1) > $THRESHOLD
union
  select 'no rows'
  from v\$session
  where status='ACTIVE'
  having count(1) <= $THRESHOLD;
  spool off
  exit
EOF
RETURN_CODE=`grep "Threshold" $LOGFILE | wc -l`
if [ $RETURN_CODE -eq 0 ]
  then
 exit 0
else
 exit 1
fi
```

Upon being notified that the active session count is high in your instance, the next step is to determine what caused the unexpected increase in the number of active sessions. Often this may occur when one or more sessions are consuming a lot of system resources. This can cause a bottle-neck in the system, causing other sessions in the database to remain in an active state because they are unable to get enough resources to complete. (Assessing high CPU consuming queries is discussed in the following section.) Sometimes you may see high active sessions due to one-time processing or increased overall activity in your database.

Communicate with your user community to understand what processing may be occurring that is not normally scheduled. Also, get an understanding of usage requirements if you notice upward or downward trends in database sessions.

■**Tip** The high active sessions threshold should be periodically evaluated to determine whether it is still relevant to your organization. Database trends should be evaluated.

Identifying High CPU Consuming Sessions

A typical cause of high active sessions in the database is when one or more active sessions are consuming a large amount of CPU. You can identify such sessions by executing the following query:

```
select ss.sid,ss.value CPU ,se.username,se.program
from v$sesstat ss, v$session se
where ss.statistic# in
(select statistic#
from v$statname
where name = 'CPU used by this session')
and se.sid=ss.sid
and ss.sid>6 -- disregard background processes
order by CPU;
```

■**Note** It is difficult to proactively monitor high CPU consuming sessions—there are often sessions that simply require a large amount of CPU resources in order to process, which makes determining a threshold for this condition very complex. Often other symptoms arise that alert the Applications DBA to look for sessions of this nature, so only a query for sorting for high CPU consumers is provided.

To resolve the issue of high CPU consumption, you may need to remove the offending session to free resources for the other sessions in the database. If the troubling database session is an ad hoc query, Concurrent Manager job, or Forms session, it may be possible to cancel the process from within the application. Large resource consuming sessions could also arise from poorly written custom queries, bugs in application code, invalid database statistics, or a corrupt index. Additional research will be required to determine the root cause. Be certain that preventative maintenance tasks are executing properly (these are outlined in Chapter 6 of this guide).

The solution to the high consuming session may involve an application patch, query rewrite, gathering statistics, or rebuilding indexes. If the process is simply a long running process, it may be scheduled after hours or run against a reporting database. The primary concern is to ensure the responsiveness of the business transactions.

■**Tip** When canceling a session from the application, it is also recommended that you verify that the underlying database operating system process has been cancelled.

Identifying large CPU consuming sessions may also be achieved by sorting active sessions by CPU usage in EM 10*g* Grid Control. Operating system commands, such as top and ps, may also be used to display the top consumers. Additional information about identifying high CPU consuming sessions is included in Chapter 4 of this guide.

Monitoring Total Session Count

The Applications DBA may want to be notified when the total number of sessions in the database approaches the maximum allowed for your organization. This is typically monitored in order to assure licensing compliance. Applications DBAs should be aware of increases in session counts, as each session requires additional system resources.

The following script can be used to monitor the total number of sessions in the database:

```
#This script is used to monitor the total number of sessions
#THRESHOLD is the maximum number of sessions
#that may be connected to the database at one time
THRESHOLD=$1
LOGFILE=/tmp/high_sessions_$ORACLE_SID.txt
sqlplus -s apps/apps << EOF
  set heading off
  spool $LOGFILE
  select '$ORACLE_SID - High Session Threshold - '||count(1)
  from v\$session
  having count(1) > $THRESHOLD
union
  select 'no rows'
  from v\$session
  having count(1) <= $THRESHOLD;
  spool off
  exit
```

```
EOF
RETURN_CODE=`grep "Threshold" $LOGFILE | wc -l`
if [ $RETURN_CODE -eq 0 ]
  then
  exit 0
else
  exit 1
fi
```

A high number of sessions may indicate that sessions are not disconnecting from the database properly. This issue can be monitored in conjunction with the long idle session monitoring discussed previously in the "Identifying Long Idle Sessions" section of this chapter.

■**Tip** It is common for Oracle 11*i* applications to have a high number of JDBC Thin Client connections in the database. A periodic bounce of the Apache Server is recommended to release JDBC thin client sessions that do not gracefully disconnect. A script for performing an Apache Server bounce will be provided in the Chapter 6 of this guide.

Identifying Long Running Sessions

Another type of problem database session is one that has been running for an unusually long period of time. This type of session may cause problems with resource contention when transaction activity increases.

The following query will monitor long running sessions:

```
#This script is used to monitor long running sessions
#Threshold is the number of days a session may be active
#in the database. For example, for an 36 hour threshold use 1.5.
THRESHOLD=$1
LOGFILE=/tmp/long_running_$ORACLE_SID.log
sqlplus -s apps/apps << EOF
  set heading off
  spool $LOGFILE
  select distinct '$ORACLE_SID - Long Running Sessions above
Threshold.'
  from v\$session db_session,
    v\$process process,
    v\$session_wait wait
  where process.addr = db_session.paddr
    and db_session.sid = wait.sid
```

```
  and type='USER'
  and db_session.username is not null
  and db_session.username not in ('SYS', 'SYSTEM')
  and db_session.program not like 'JDBC%'
  and logon_time<(sysdate - $THRESHOLD);
-- add data to logfile
select db_session.username,
  db_session.osuser,
  db_session.terminal,
  wait.event,
  db_session.program,
  db_session.status,
  to_char(logon_time,'dd-mm-yy hh:mi am') "LOGON"
from v\$session db_session,
  v\$process process,
  v\$session_wait wait
where process.addr = db_session.paddr
  and db_session.sid = wait.sid
  and type='USER'
  and db_session.username is not null
  and db_session.username not in ('SYS', 'SYSTEM')
  and db_session.program not like 'JDBC%'
  and logon_time<(sysdate - $THRESHOLD)
order by logon_time;
spool off
exit
EOF
RETURN_CODE=`grep "Threshold" $LOGFILE | wc -l`
if [ $RETURN_CODE -eq 0 ]
  then
 exit 0
else
 exit 1
fi
```

In this script, the query ignores the SYS and SYSTEM users, as well as JDBC
Thin Client sessions. These are ignored because SYS and SYSTEM will often
have valid long running sessions. Additionally, JDBC Thin Client sessions are
activated when the iAS is started, so extended JDBC Thin Client sessions are
normal for Oracle applications. The script may be customized to exclude certain users or certain types of programs, depending on your requirements.

Once long running sessions have been identified, you should contact
the user of the session and determine whether the process should still be
executing. If it should not be running, the session should be killed.

Identifying Blocking Sessions

An Applications DBA should also monitor for database blocking sessions. A blocking session is one that has a lock on a resource that is required by another session; therefore, the session is blocking the processing of another session.

The following query returns the database session ID or sid if there is a blocking session:

```
#This script is used to monitor for blocking sessions
LOGFILE=/tmp/blocking_$ORACLE_SID.txt
sqlplus -s apps/apps << EOF
  set heading off
  spool $LOGFILE
  select sid
  from v\$lock
  where block > 0;
  spool off
  exit
EOF
RETURN_CODE=`grep "no rows" $LOGFILE | wc -l`
if [ $RETURN_CODE -eq 0 ]
  then
  exit 0
else
  exit 1
fi
```

When this situation is encountered, the Applications DBA should contact the blocking user and ask that the transaction be completed or cancelled, or the DBA can simply kill the blocking session.

■**Note** Database and listener availability monitoring as well as session monitoring is available in the EM 10*g* Grid Control Diagnostics Pack. There are many other third-party tools that can assist with this level of monitoring as well.

Storage Monitoring

By monitoring for database storage issues, the Applications DBA can typically resolve space constraints before users encounter failures. The Applications DBA should proactively monitor the following storage conditions:

- Tablespace sizing limitations (when objects cannot extend)
- Datafile extent limitations (when a datafile has hit a threshold close to its maximum size)
- Object maximum extent limitations (when a segment has hit a threshold close to its maximum number of extents)

Identifying Tablespace Sizing Limitations

A common space-management error that can be encountered by users is the ORA-03232 error. This error indicates that there is not enough free space in the tablespace for the database object to acquire another extent. The Applications DBA can proactively monitor for this occurrence by using the following query to check the free space available for each object's next extent:

```
#Script used to identify objects for sizing limitations
LOGFILE=/tmp/extent_room_$ORACLE_SID.log
sqlplus -s apps/apps << EOF
  set heading off
  spool $LOGFILE
  select distinct '$ORACLE_SID - Threshold - Not enough space for
next extent.'
  from dba_segments a
  where not exists (select 'x'
      from dba_free_space b
      where a.tablespace_name = b.tablespace_name
          and b.bytes > a.next_extent);
  -- add data to logfile
  select tablespace_name,
    owner,
    segment_name,
    segment_type,
    to_char((next_extent/1024),'999,999')||'K' next_extent_size
  from dba_segments a
  where not exists (select 'x'
      from dba_free_space b
      where a.tablespace_name = b.tablespace_name
          and b.bytes > a.next_extent)
  order by tablespace_name,segment_name;
  spool off
  exit
EOF
RETURN_CODE=`grep "Threshold" $LOGFILE | wc -l`
```

```
if [ $RETURN_CODE -eq 0 ]
  then
  exit 0
else
  exit 1
fi
```

In order to resolve this issue, you need to allocate more space to the tablespace. This can be accomplished by increasing the size of the datafile, setting the datafiles of the object's tablespace to AUTOEXTEND, or adding more datafiles to the tablespace.

The following statement will alter a datafile to automatically extend:

```
alter tablespace [tablespace_name]
datafile '[path/datafile_name]' autoextend;
```

The following statement will alter a datafile to extend to a given size:

```
alter tablespace [tablespace_name]
datafile '[path/datafile_name]' size [size]M;
```

The following statement will add a datafile to the tablespace:

```
alter tablespace [tablespace_name] add
datafile '[path/datafile_name]' size [size]M;
```

■**Note** In the preceding statements, [tablespace_name] is the name of the tablespace, [path/datafile_name] is the path and name of the datafile, and [size] is the size to extend the datafile to, or the size of the new datafile.

When possible, uniform extents should be used when the tablespace is created. If an object is dropped, the space held by that object will be more easily reused if the extents are uniform among all objects (thus assisting in avoiding extent allocation issues). Also, the pct_increase tablespace parameter should be set to 0. If pct_increase is set to a value greater than 0, the object will try to obtain larger and larger extents, which makes reusing the space upon deletion of segments more difficult.

■**Tip** Even if a datafile is configured with the AUTOEXTEND option, datafile growth is always restricted by the amount of free space available on the filesystem. Proactively monitoring filesystem space usage is discussed in the "Server Filesystem Usage" section later in this chapter.

Identifying Datafile Extent Limitations

Datafiles may also have limitations on their ability to extend. When datafiles are set with the AUTOEXTEND option, you may also encounter errors with extent allocation if the datafile is unable to extend because it is close to its set maximum size. This can occur due to operating system limitations that restrict the size of your datafiles, so you will need to periodically add datafiles to the tablespace even if the datafiles are set to automatically extend.

To monitor for datafiles that are near their maximum number of extents, the Applications DBA can use the following script:

```
#Script used to monitor datafiles close to their maximum size
#Threshold is number of extents away from the maximum datafile size
THRESHOLD=$1
LOGFILE=/tmp/datafile_extents_$ORACLE_SID.log
sqlplus -s apps/apps << EOF
  set heading off
  spool $LOGFILE
  select distinct '$ORACLE_SID - Threshold for datafiles near max
extents'
  from dba_data_files
  where autoextensible='YES'
    and trunc((maxblocks-blocks) /increment_by) <= $THRESHOLD
    and increment_by != 0 ;
  -- add data to logfile
  select file_name, trunc((maxblocks-blocks) /increment_by)
  from dba_data_files
  where autoextensible='YES'
    and trunc((maxblocks-blocks) /increment_by) <= $THRESHOLD
    and increment_by != 0;
  spool off
  exit
```

```
EOF
RETURN_CODE=`grep "Threshold" $LOGFILE | wc -l`
if [ $RETURN_CODE -eq 0 ]
  then
  exit 0
else
  exit 1
fi
```

If datafiles are near their maximum size, either the maximum size of the datafile needs to be increased, or one or more datafiles need to be added to the tablespace. The commands for both of these solutions were outlined in the previous "Identifying Tablespace Sizing Limitations" section.

■**Caution** Be aware of operating system limitations that are associated with large files. If your filesystems can support large files, you can set each datafile to have a maximum size larger than 2GB. You should review and understand the limitations that may be associated with your flavor and version of UNIX. Some limitations you should review are filesystem configuration options for supporting large files and limitations of commands that manipulate and move files, such as `tar`.

Identifying Maximum Extent Limitations

Even if plenty of space is available within the tablespace, errors can be encountered due to an object reaching its maximum number of extents. To monitor for objects at a threshold near the maximum number of extents, the Applications DBA can use the following script:

```
#Script used to monitor objects that are close to
#their max number of extents
#Threshold is number of extents from the maximum
THRESHOLD=$1
LOGFILE=/tmp/max_extents_$ORACLE_SID.log
sqlplus -s apps/apps << EOF
  set heading off
  spool $LOGFILE
  select distinct '$ORACLE_SID - Threshold for objects near max
extents'
  from dba_segments
  where max_extents - extents <= $THRESHOLD;
```

```
-- add data to logfile
select owner,
  segment_name,
  segment_type,
  tablespace_name,
  extents,
  max_extents
from dba_segments
where max_extents - extents <= $THRESHOLD
order by extents DESC;
spool off
exit
EOF
RETURN_CODE=`grep "Threshold" $LOGFILE | wc -l`
if [ $RETURN_CODE -eq 0 ]
 then
 exit 0
else
 exit 1
fi
```

To resolve this problem, you can alter the segment to increase the maximum number of extents allowed. This can be achieved by executing the following command:

```
alter [object_type] [object_name] storage (maxextents [number]);
```

In this command, [object_type] is either table or index, [object_name] is the name of the object, and [number] is the maximum number of extents. The following is a specific example of the alter statement that sets the maximum number of extents to 500 for the table FND_USERS:

```
SQL>alter table FND_USERS storage (maxextents 500);
```

If the object is exhibiting fast growth, the extent size setting may be too low. If this is the case, you may also set the maximum number of extents to UNLIMITED, thus avoiding this error in the future. This is accomplished by specifying UNLIMITED in the storage clause. The following is an example of setting the maximum number of extents to UNLIMITED for the FND_USERS tables:

```
SQL>alter table FND_USERS storage (maxextents UNLIMITED);
```

Apache Server Monitoring and Troubleshooting

Monitoring the Web Node involves monitoring the Apache server provided with iAS and monitoring the Java servlets. Troubleshooting tasks consist of configuration validation steps and log file research.

Apache Log Files

When troubleshooting Apache, the Applications DBA should monitor the various log files for Apache and the JServs. The $APACHE_TOP/Apache/logs directory contains files such as error_log and error_log_pls. The JServ log files are located in the $APACHE_TOP/Apache/Jserv/logs and $APACHE_TOP/Apache/Jserv/logs/jvm directories. Apache and JServ log files should be monitored for potential error messages.

To enable additional logging for Apache when you're troubleshooting, you can modify the level of debug messaging in the jserv.log file. The location of the jserv.log file is defined by the log.file parameter in the jserv.properties file. These are the steps for enabling the additional logging:

1. Set LogLevel to DEBUG in $APACHE_TOP/Apache/conf/httpd.conf.

2. Set ApJservLogLevel to DEBUG in $APACHE_TOP/Jserv/etc/jserv.conf.

3. Make the following changes to $APACHE_TOP/Jserv/etc/jserv.properties:

   • Add wrapper.bin.parameters=-Djbo.debugoutput=console

   • Set log=true

   • Set log.channel=true

   • Set log.channel.info=true

   • Set log.channel.debug=true

Once these changes are made, review the log files for information to assist with troubleshooting the underlying issue. Use the information from the log files to search MetaLink for issue resolution. If MetaLink does not provide you with solutions, you should open an SR with Oracle Support.

You can also create a log file for iProcurement debugging in the directory and file specified by the debug_output parameter. To do so, make the following changes to $APACHE_TOP/Jserv/etc/ssp_init.txt:

- Set debug_level=5
- Set debug_output=[path/file]
- Set debug_switch=ON

The log file created with these modifications can be used to assist in resolving issues with iProcurement. Information obtained from the log files may be used to research MetaLink or to open an SR with Oracle Support.

■**Tip** Be certain to turn off or reset the logging values when the troubleshooting process has completed; otherwise unnecessary logging could cause performance degradation and potentially fill up a filesystem.

Apache Availability

Monitoring of Apache processes will allow the Applications DBA to respond as quickly as possible to a major outage. This will assist in minimizing unplanned downtime for the system.

The following script can be used to monitor for Apache availability:

```
#Script used to monitor Apache Server availability
LOGFILE=/tmp/apache_updown.log
adapcctl.sh status
if [ $? -eq 1 ]
  then
     echo "$ORACLE_SID - Apache is down" > $LOGFILE
     exit 1
  else
     exit 0
fi
```

If the Apache Server becomes unavailable, you should monitor the log files, as described in the previous section, to assist in determining the cause of the failure. If necessary, research potential causes on MetaLink, or log an SR to assist with resolving the issue.

Troubleshooting iAS Configuration

There are several tools available to assist with troubleshooting iAS configuration. The most comprehensive tool is the AOL/J Test. This tool can be accessed directly with a URL, and as of Framework version 5.10 it is also available through menu options in OAM.

■**Note** Additional details regarding AOL/J Test can be found in MetaLink Note 275875.1.

To access the AOL/J Test tool directly, the following URL may be used:

`http://<hostname>:<port>/OA_HTML/jsp/fnd/aoljtest.jsp`

JavaServer Pages (JSP) will prompt for the following information:

- APPS username
- APPS password
- Database SID
- Database host name
- Database listener port

Enter the requested information, and click the Test button to continue. The program will establish a connection to the database and return a screen with the Java version and `classpath` environment settings. From this screen, the user can select a link to Enter AOL/J Setup Test, which takes you to the page displayed in Figure 3-1.

The AOL/J Setup Tests page can be used to verify DBC file settings, display and test the Web Agent settings, display and test the Servlet Agent settings, and test X Server access. (X Server is used for dynamic GIF file generation, among other things.)

To access the AOL/J Test tool with OAM, log in to the application, pick the System Administration responsibility, and then click on the AOL/J test you wish to perform from the Diagnostics menu options, as shown in Figure 3-2.

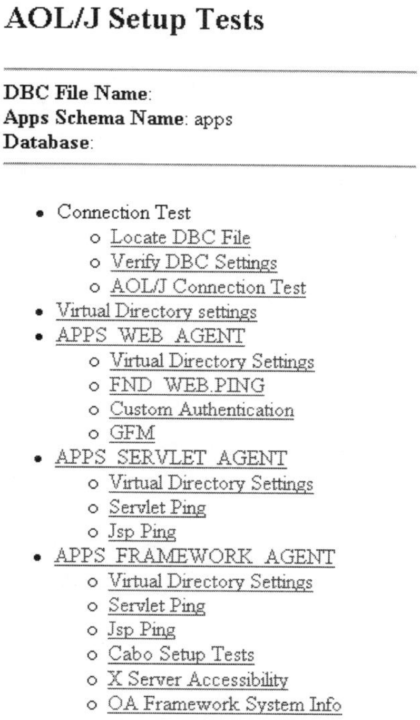

AOL/J Setup Tests

DBC File Name:
Apps Schema Name: apps
Database:

- Connection Test
    - Locate DBC File
    - Verify DBC Settings
    - AOL/J Connection Test
- Virtual Directory settings
- APPS_WEB_AGENT
    - Virtual Directory Settings
    - FND_WEB.PING
    - Custom Authentication
    - GFM
- APPS_SERVLET_AGENT
    - Virtual Directory Settings
    - Servlet Ping
    - Jsp Ping
- APPS_FRAMEWORK_AGENT
    - Virtual Directory Settings
    - Servlet Ping
    - Jsp Ping
    - Cabo Setup Tests
    - X Server Accessibility
    - OA Framework System Info

Figure 3-1. *AOL/J test menu options*

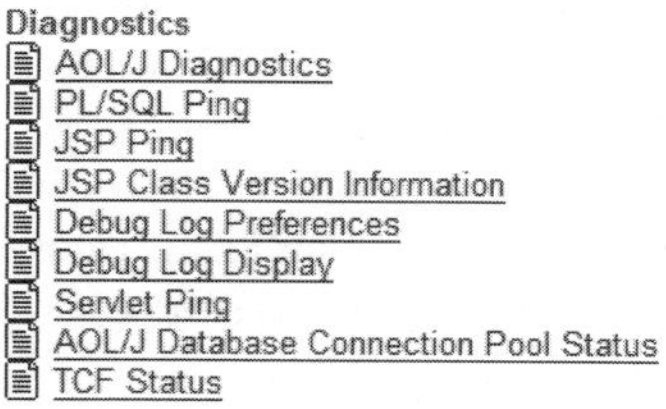

Diagnostics
▤ AOL/J Diagnostics
▤ PL/SQL Ping
▤ JSP Ping
▤ JSP Class Version Information
▤ Debug Log Preferences
▤ Debug Log Display
▤ Servlet Ping
▤ AOL/J Database Connection Pool Status
▤ TCF Status

Figure 3-2. *Diagnostics menu for the System Administration responsibility*

Testing Java Servlet Configuration

When diagnosing issues with the Apache Server configuration, you may also want to validate the Java servlet configuration. To do so, access the following URL:

```
http://[host:port]/oa_servlets/oracle.pps.fnd.text.HelloWorldServlet
```

The parameter [hostname] is the name of the node where the Java servlet is defined; the parameter [port] is the port of the Java servlet to be tested. If Java servlets are properly defined, this URL will return a "Hello World" message in your browser.

The same task may be accomplished by accessing the Diagnostics ➤ Servlet Ping menu in OAM.

Monitoring the JVM Pool

If memory issues are identified in the JServ log files, the Applications DBA should monitor the JVM connection pool with the Application Module (AM) Pool Monitor. This will assist in redefining memory settings for the JServ.

Prior to Framework 5.10, JVM connection pools could be monitored with the following link:

```
http://[hostname]:[port]/servlets/OAAppModPoolMonitor
```

With the 5.10 Framework, this link is invalid, and the global Diagnostics button or OAM is the source for this information instead. In order for the global Diagnostics option to be available, the profile FND: Diagnostic must be set to Yes. Access the AM Pool Monitor in OAM by selecting Site Map ➤ Monitoring ➤ JServ Usage from the menu, and then clicking on the AM Pools tab.

However you initiate it, the AM Pool Monitor will provide links for information related to JVM settings, JVM memory consumption, BC4J settings, servlet sessions, and the Application Module Pool.

Forms Monitoring and Troubleshooting

You can monitor Forms by using functionality in OAM and by viewing log files on the Forms Node. With OAM, the Applications DBA can view information regarding active SQL being run by the Form and performance statistics for that session.

Using OAM

OAM Minipack version H has many features for monitoring Forms activity. Forms-monitoring features can be accessed from Site Map ➤ Monitoring ➤ Current Activity. The menu options include Forms Sessions and Forms Runtime Processes.

OAM will display Forms users through the Forms Sessions screen, which displays statistics such as Logical Reads, CPU, and Duration. This screen has a Session Details button to allow viewing of the associated SQL statement, and detailed Session Wait information.

The Forms Runtime Processes screen shown in Figure 3-3 allows the Applications DBA to view the sessions related to a Forms process. To do this, select the desired Forms session and click the Sessions button.

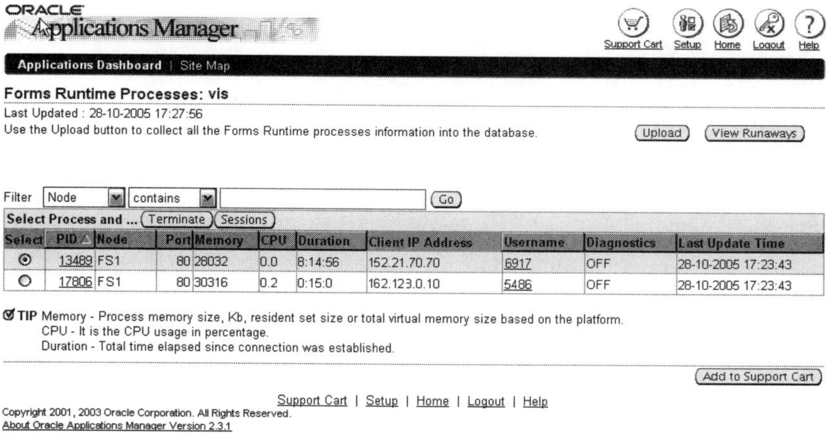

Figure 3-3. *The Forms Runtime Processes screen in OAM*

From the Forms Runtime Processes screen, the Applications DBA may also click the View Runaways button. The following runaway process thresholds may be filtered (so you can view information about the Forms processes that meet your criteria): maximum memory, maximum CPU, and maximum duration. From this screen you also have the option to terminate a process by selecting it and clicking the Terminate button.

Monitoring Forms Dump Files

Forms Server dump files are created on the Forms Node. These files are created in the directory where the Forms process was started. The dump files are named f60webmx_dump_xxxx, where xxxx is a process number. Monitoring should be set up for the directory where these files are created. Notifications can be sent to the appropriate staff if there is an excessive number of dump files created.

The following script can be used to monitor for Forms dump files:

```
#Script used to monitor creation of forms dump files
FORMS_DIR=$1
LOGFILE=/tmp/forms_dumpfiles_$ORACLE_SID.log

ls -l $FORMS_DIR/f60webmx_dump* > $LOGFILE
if [ $? -eq 0 ]
 then
    # There are dump files, return an error code
    exit 1
else
    exit 0
fi
```

If dump files are generated for Forms sessions, the dump files should be reviewed for additional information that can be used to perform research in MetaLink or open an SR to resolve the underlying issue.

It may also be necessary to generate Forms trace files. Steps for generating Forms trace files are included in Chapter 4 of this guide.

Concurrent Manager Monitoring

Given the size and complexity of many of the jobs run by the Concurrent Manager, there is always the potential for problems with submitted concurrent requests. Likewise, a resource-intensive Concurrent Manager request can result in database performance issues. Due to the criticality of concurrent processing, the Applications DBA needs to monitor it closely.

This section will cover the following topics:

- Monitoring Concurrent Manager log and output files
- Reviewing active concurrent requests
- Monitoring pending concurrent requests
- Canceling active concurrent requests and removing underlying database and operating system processes

Monitoring Concurrent Manager Log Files

The Concurrent Manager log and output files are located in the $APPLCSF/ $APPLLOG and $APPLCSF/$APPLOUT directories. Errors encountered during the job processing will be written to these files, and it is the responsibility of the user who submits a request to monitor the concurrent request log and output files for errors.

The Applications DBA should be aware of the location of the log and output files and be able to assist in resolving issues if necessary.

Reviewing Active Concurrent Requests

The Applications DBA can view running concurrent requests through OAM or by using the afcmrrq.sql script. This script is provided with Oracle Applications and must be executed as the APPS user on the Admin Node as follows:

```
SQL>@$FND_TOP/sql/afcmrrq
```

Active concurrent requests may also be viewed with OAM by selecting Site Map ➤ Administration ➤ Concurrent Requests ➤ Running from the menu, as shown in Figure 3-4.

Concurrent Requests
Submit New
Pending
Running
Completed (Last Hour)

Figure 3-4. *Finding running concurrent requests with OAM*

Monitoring Pending Concurrent Requests

The Applications DBA should monitor pending concurrent requests. A high number of pending requests could alert you to issues with Concurrent Manager processing.

The following script may be used to monitor pending concurrent requests:

```
#Script used to monitor pending concurrent requests
#Threshold is the number of pending concurrent requests that is
#the maximum acceptable before triggering the alert
THRESHOLD=$1
LOGFILE=/tmp/pending_requests_$ORACLE_SID.txt
sqlplus -s apps/apps << EOF
  set heading off
  spool $LOGFILE
```

```
select '$ORACLE_SID - Pending Requests Past '||
  'Threshold - '||count(1)
from fnd_concurrent_requests
where phase_code='p'
having count(1) > $THRESHOLD
union
  select 'no rows'
  from fnd_concurrent_requests
  where  phase_code='p'
  having count(1) <= $THRESHOLD;
  spool off
  exit
EOF
RETURN_CODE=`grep "Threshold" $LOGFILE | wc -l`
if [ $RETURN_CODE -eq 0 ]
  then
  exit 0
else
  exit 1
fi
```

You may also view the number of pending concurrent requests with OAM. There are several paths for displaying pending concurrent requests; the simplest is to select Site Map ➤ Administration ➤ Concurrent Request. From here simply select the Pending Requests menu option, displayed previously in Figure 3-4.

To resolve issues with a high number of pending concurrent requests, you will need to determine the bottleneck for the requests. It is possible that a resource-intensive request has been submitted or a poor-performing request. You may need to research MetaLink or log an SR to resolve the issue.

Canceling Active Concurrent Requests

If a user is going to cancel a resource-intensive concurrent request, it is helpful to obtain the database session ID or sid for that process. The following query will return this information for a given concurrent request ID:

```
select r.request_id "Request ID",
   s.sid "Session ID" ,
   g.concurrent_program_name "Concurrent Program"
from applsys.fnd_concurrent_requests r,
   applsys.fnd_concurrent_queues_tl qt,
   applsys.fnd_concurrent_queues q,
   applsys.fnd_concurrent_processes p,
```

```
applsys.fnd_concurrent_programs g,
v$session s
where r.controlling_manager=p.concurrent_process_id
   and q.application_id=p.queue_application_id
   and q.concurrent_queue_id=p.concurrent_queue_id
   and qt.application_id=q.application_id
   and qt.concurrent_queue_id=q.concurrent_queue_id
   and r.phase_code='R'
   and qt.language in ('US')
   and p.session_id=s.audsid
   and g.concurrent_program_id = r.concurrent_program_id
   and r.request_id = &request_id
```

The database sid can be used to kill the database session if it does not terminate when the request is canceled within the application. In these cases, the application and the afcmrrq.sql script will not show that the request is running, but the database session will remain active. If the database session is not removed, performance problems may occur as a result of the resources being consumed by this session.

Database and operating system information for a running concurrent request may also be obtained from OAM. The simplest way to get this information is to select Site Map ➤ Administration ➤ Concurrent Requests ➤ Running. From this list of running concurrent requests, select the AUDSID to obtain additional information regarding the session. This information includes the operating system's process ID (Oracle SPID) and the database sid (Session ID).

Monitoring Concurrent Request Run Times

Periodically the Applications DBA should check on the Concurrent Manager metrics. It is useful to generate a report of short running requests that spend time waiting. If there are many short running jobs that are unable to begin due to resource contention with long running jobs, the Applications DBA may need to look into creating an additional Concurrent Manager to service these requests.

Long running jobs should also be monitored. If certain long running jobs take an increasingly long amount of time to process, there may be a tuning opportunity for that job. This will also allow the Applications DBA to prevent the potential problem of the job taking so long to complete that it interferes with other jobs. Within the long running jobs report, the Applications DBA should look for jobs that suddenly appear on the list. These may be jobs that are suddenly taking longer due to a significant data change or bug introduced into the program. The investigation process for this issue may require opening an SR with Oracle Support.

OAM provides an easy method for generating reports regarding short running and long running requests. From the menu, select Site Map ➤ Monitoring ➤ Current Activity ➤ Concurrent Requests. Then click on the Advanced Search button. The options available from this screen will include Waiting Requests by Time, Short Running Requests that Waited, and Long Running Requests, as displayed in Figure 3-5.

By Duration/Wait time

```
○ Waiting Requests by Time                           ○ Long Running Requests
        Maximum Wait Time  [        ] [ Minutes ▼ ]
        Minimum Wait Time  [        ] [ Minutes ▼ ]          Minimum Duration  [        ] [ Minutes ▼ ]
○ Short Running Requests that Waited
        Maximum Duration   [        ] [ Minutes ▼ ]    ⦿ None of the above
        Minimum Wait Time  [        ] [ Minutes ▼ ]
```

Quick Searches:

Requests submitted in the last one hour
Pending Requests submitted in the last 24 hours
Errored Requests submitted in the last 24 hours
Completed Requests in the last 24 hours that ran for more than 60 minutes

Figure 3-5. *Advanced searches for concurrent requests*

■**Tip** Concurrent Manager reports are available with the Applications Pack for Enterprise Manager 10*g*. The information provided by these reports is useful for tuning Concurrent Managers.

Server Monitoring and Troubleshooting

The servers running each node should be monitored for server availability, CPU usage, and filesystem usage. Additional monitoring may be implemented as needed.

Server Availability

The most basic monitoring for the server checks whether the server is available. The following script may be executed from any server other than the server being monitored, to determine if it is available:

```
#Script used to monitor server availability
SERVER_NAME=$1
LOGFILE=/tmp/server_check_$SERVER_NAME.txt
ping -c1 $SERVER_NAME
if [ $? -eq 1 ]
   then
```

```
    echo "Server $SERVER_NAME is unreachable" > $LOGFILE
    exit 1
else
    exit 0
fi
```

If the server becomes unavailable, you should contact your UNIX system administrator to assist in troubleshooting the cause of the failure. At times, an inaccessible server is due to networking issues. Once the server is again online, you should verify that the database and application are functioning properly. If your database server was down, it may be necessary to bounce components of the Oracle Application to reestablish connectivity from the different nodes to the database.

■**Note** A multi-server environment will assist in providing high availability if server failure occurs. For example, if you have a web farm that consists of four Web Servers, and one Web Server crashes, the others are still available. The same holds true if you have multiple Concurrent Processing Nodes and multiple clustered nodes in an Oracle RAC implementation for the database. Multi-server architectures provide higher availability for your applications. For more information regarding multi-server implementations, see Chapter 1 of this guide.

Server CPU Utilization

It is also important for the Applications DBA to monitor the CPU usage of the servers. The threshold for CPU utilization is site specific, but a general rule of thumb for CPU usage is to keep the server at no less than 20 percent idle for an extended period of time.

The following script will monitor CPU usage:

```
#Script used to monitor server CPU utilization
#Threshold is the maximum percentage of CPU utilization acceptable
THRESHOLD=$1
TMPFILE=/tmp/tmp_cpu.txt
LOGFILE=/tmp/cpu_utilization.log
HOSTNAME=`hostname`
vmstat 2 2 > $TMPFILE
IDLE_TIME=`tail -1 $TMPFILE | awk '{ print $16 }'`
if [ $IDLE_TIME -gt $THRESHOLD ]
    then
        exit 0
```

```
else
    echo "$HOSTNAME - Server CPU utilization High" > $LOGFILE
    exit 1
fi
```

High CPU consumption is sometimes a symptom of underlying performance issues or a long running job. If your server experiences numerous periods of high CPU utilization, it is possible that additional processing power is required for the server. Additional information about tuning CPU consumption is provided in Chapter 4 of this guide.

Server Memory Utilization

It is also important for the Applications DBA to monitor the memory usage of the servers. The threshold for memory utilization is also site specific.

The following script will monitor server memory utilization:

```
#Script used to monitor server memory utilization
#Threshold is the maximum percentage of memory used
THRESHOLD=$1
TMPFILE=/tmp/tmp_mem.txt
LOGFILE=/tmp/memory_utilization.log
HOSTNAME=`hostname`
sar -r 2 2 > $TMPFILE
MEM_USAGE=`tail -1 $TMPFILE | awk '{ print $4 }'`
if [ $MEM_USAGE -gt $THRESHOLD ]
    then
        echo "$HOSTNAME - Server Memory utilization High - $MEM_USAGE" >
$LOGFILE
        exit 1
    else
        exit 0
fi
```

Like high CPU utilization, high memory consumption is sometimes a symptom of underlying performance issues or a long running job. If your server frequently experiences low memory, it is possible that additional memory is required. Additional information for resolving high memory consumption is provided in Chapter 4 of this guide.

Server Filesystem Usage

Filesystem monitoring should focus on the amount of free space available. If database datafiles are set to AUTOEXTEND, the filesystem containing them should have sufficient free disk space to allow for extents.

Other filesystems to monitor include the filesystem where the database bdump and udump directories are located. If the database is running in ARCHIVELOG mode, the filesystem where the archive logs are written should also be monitored. The archive log filesystem may require a higher threshold for space usage monitoring. If a data-intensive process is planned to occur, the threshold may need to be changed in order to prevent any problems, such as the database hanging due to the archive directory running out of space.

Middle tier nodes will also benefit from filesystem monitoring. Apache log files, JServ log files, and Concurrent Manager output and log files can consume large amounts of disk space. By being notified of potential storage issues, the Applications DBA can prevent such errors.

The following script can be used to monitor filesystems on the server:

```
#Script used to monitor filesystem free space
#Threshold is amount of free MB for the filesystem
THRESHOLD=$1
FILESYSTEM=$2
LOGFILE=/tmp/space_avail_$FILESYSTEM.log
HOSTNAME=`hostname`
AVAILABLE=`df -m /$FILESYSTEM | grep $FILESYSTEM | awk '{print $3}'`
if [ $AVAILABLE -gt $THRESHOLD ]
   then
      exit 0
else
      echo exit 1 "$HOSTNAME - $FILESYSTEM threshold $THRESHOLD
exceeded" > $LOGFILE
fi
```

If the filesystem space usage alert is triggered, the Applications DBA should ask the UNIX system administrator to increase the space allocated to the filesystem.

Network Monitoring

Monitoring and troubleshooting network issues can be done with client-level commands or through using an application form. This section will provide information regarding the following tools that are available for network monitoring and troubleshooting:

- Using ping and tracert, two very useful operating system commands for monitoring networking issues

- Performing a network trace from a Forms session to detect network latency issues

---

■**Note** This section will outline the tools available, but it will not provide specifics on how to resolve network latency issues. If any such issues occur, contact your network administrator for assistance.

Using ping and tracert for Network Monitoring

There are several operating system commands that can be used for troubleshooting network issues. From the client experiencing problems, issuing commands such as ping or tracert can provide valuable information.

The ping command will demonstrate whether the client has access to the node. Without access to the node, the user will be unable to access the Oracle E-Business Suite application. Assuming that the application is accessed through the URL https://vis.domain.com, the user must be able to access the address vis.domain.com. If access exists, the ping command should return the following:

```
C:\> ping vis.domain.com
```

```
Pinging vis.domain.com [127.0.0.1] with 32 bytes of data:

Reply from 127.0.0.1: bytes=32 time=39ms TTL=53
Reply from 127.0.0.1: bytes=32 time=41ms TTL=53
Reply from 127.0.0.1: bytes=32 time=38ms TTL=53
Reply from 127.0.0.1: bytes=32 time=54ms TTL=53

Ping statistics for 127.0.0.1:
    Packets: Sent = 4, Received = 4, Lost = 0 (0% loss),
Approximate round trip times in milli-seconds:
    Minimum = 38ms, Maximum = 54ms, Average = 43ms
```

Some useful troubleshooting information is provided with the results of the ping command. If the output indicates that packets are lost, there may be network issues for that client. Also, if the reply times out or takes an abnormally long time, there may be network issues. If the ping command returns the following output, there may be a problem with your Domain Name System (DNS):

```
C:\> ping vis.domain.com
```

```
Ping request could not find host vis.domain.com.  Please check
the name and try again.
```

If this error is experienced, you should contact a networking specialist in your organization to resolve the issue.

■**Tip** It is helpful to keep a list of the IP addresses of your hosts. These can be used to establish connections if there is a DNS problem at your site.

Another useful network command is tracert. This command will show the network path taken to connect to a particular domain. The information returned by tracert can provide useful information about connection time. Here is an example:

```
C:\>tracert www.domain.com
```

```
Tracing route to www.domain.com [69.7.239.163]
over a maximum of 30 hops:
  1    32 ms    12 ms    22 ms  10.7.104.1
  2    13 ms    63 ms    45 ms  12-220-8-59.client.insightBB.com ➥
[12.220.8.59]
  3   253 ms   217 ms   241 ms  12-220-1-154.client.insightBB.com ➥
[12.220.1.154]

  4   190 ms   247 ms   248 ms  12-220-1-218.client.insightBB.com ➥
[12.220.1.218]

  5   215 ms   219 ms   201 ms  12-220-0-42.client.insightBB.com ➥
[12.220.0.42]
  6   264 ms   324 ms   396 ms  tbr1-p010901.sl9mo.ip.att.net ➥
[12.122.80.194]
  7   170 ms   202 ms   202 ms  tbr1-cl4.wswdc.ip.att.net ➥
[12.122.10.29]
  8   291 ms   323 ms   282 ms  gar1-p300.ascva.ip.att.net ➥
[12.123.8.49]
  9   101 ms   212 ms   231 ms  12.118.44.10
 10   197 ms   193 ms   253 ms  vlan260-msr2.re1.yahoo.com ➥
[216.115.96.173]
 11   261 ms   360 ms   461 ms  www.domain.com [69.7.239.163]

Trace complete.
```

Performing a Network Test from the Application

Oracle Applications also provides a Network Trace Form that the user may execute. This form is accessed by logging in to the application and choosing the Application ➤ Network Test menu option. Click the Run Test button, and the Form will return information about network latency and bandwidth. The number of iterations and trails can be customized for each execution of the test. A sample of the output is shown in Figure 3-6.

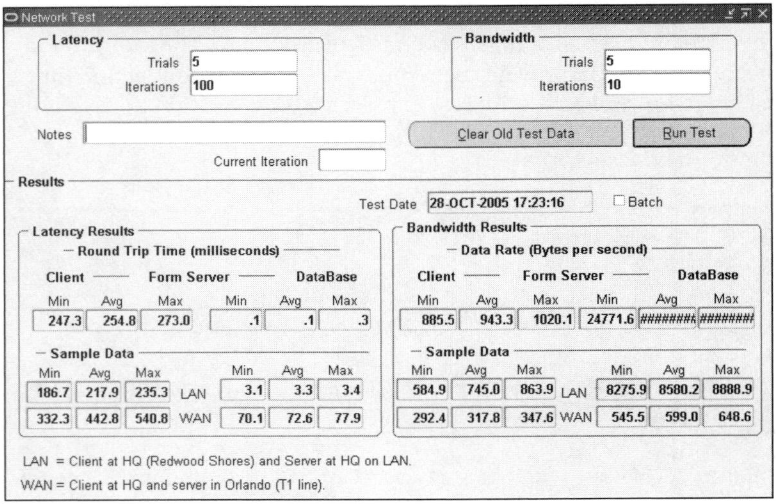

Figure 3-6. *Forms network test*

This information can be used by your company's or customer's networking team to determine whether networking bottlenecks exist.

Additional Monitoring and Troubleshooting Topics

This section will cover some miscellaneous monitoring and troubleshooting issues:

- Monitoring profile changes, which may assist with troubleshooting configuration issues

- Monitoring and validating system backups

- Troubleshooting JInitiator issues such as deleting the cache and using the Java console

Monitoring Profile Changes

Application profile settings allow for users and system administrators to customize the functionality of the E-Business Suite. As a result, altering these profile settings can sometimes have an adverse effect on the behavior of the application. The Applications DBA should make a practice of monitoring any changes to the profile settings.

Checking profile settings is especially important when performing major patching efforts, because a patch may overwrite profile options. New profile settings may also be created during the patching process. In addition to patching, the most common reason for profile changes is user error. For example, a system administrator may change a profile setting without realizing the full impact on the system.

The following script can be used to alert you to profile options changed within a specified threshold:

```
#Script used to monitor for application profile changes
#Threshold is the number of days to query for profile changes
#For example, if you set it to 7, all profile changes that
#have occurred in the past 7 days will be displayed.
THRESHOLD=$1
LOGFILE=/tmp/profile_changes_$ORACLE_SID.txt
sqlplus -s apps/apps << EOF
  set heading off
  spool $LOGFILE
  select '$ORACLE_SID - Profile Changes Past '||
    'Threshold of $THRESHOLD days - '||count(1)
  from fnd_profile_option_values
  where last_update_date > (sysdate-$THRESHOLD)
  having count(1) > $THRESHOLD
union
  select 'no rows'
  from fnd_profile_option_values
  where last_update_date <= (sysdate-$THRESHOLD)
  having count(1) <= $THRESHOLD;
  spool off
  exit
EOF
RETURN_CODE=`grep "Threshold" $LOGFILE | wc -l`
if [ $RETURN_CODE -eq 0 ]
  then
 exit 0
else
 exit 1
fi
```

OAM may also be used to display profile changes made in the Oracle application. This requires manually viewing the screen. From the Application Dashboard, in the Configuration Changes portion of the screen (shown in Figure 3-7), it is possible to see the number of profiles that have been changed in the last 24 hours. To display profile options sorted by the Last Updated date, click the number displayed next to Site Level Profile Options.

Configuration Changes (last 24 hours)
Data Retrieved: 29-09-2005 12:18:41 📑

Patches Applied	0
Site Level Profile Options	0
Applications Context Files Edited	0

Figure 3-7. *Viewing configuration changes from the OAM Dashboard*

Monitoring System Backups

The Applications DBA should set up monitoring for the database backups. If a failure occurs during the backup, the DBA should be notified so that the situation can be resolved in a timely manner. This monitoring process should be in place regardless of the backup methodology.

Some systems benefit from exporting certain objects or schemas in addition to the regular backups. These exports can be monitored for error messages within their log files. Since backups are largely environment specific, we will not attempt to address how monitoring should occur, only that it should occur.

In addition to monitoring backups, periodic restores from backups should be performed in order to confirm backup validity. Also verify that the time required to restore the instance falls within your service level agreement. This testing process should be part of your company's disaster recovery plan.

Resolving JInitiator Issues

When users encounter problems running Forms applications on their workstations, the source of the problem may be JInitiator. Troubleshooting techniques for JInitiator include the following:

- Clearing the JAR cache
- Using the Java console

Clearing the JInitiator Cache

Most JInitiator problems can be resolved by clearing the JAR cache for the program. This can be accomplished by selecting the Cache tab on the JInitiator Control Panel, shown in Figure 3-8, and clicking the Clear JAR Cache button.

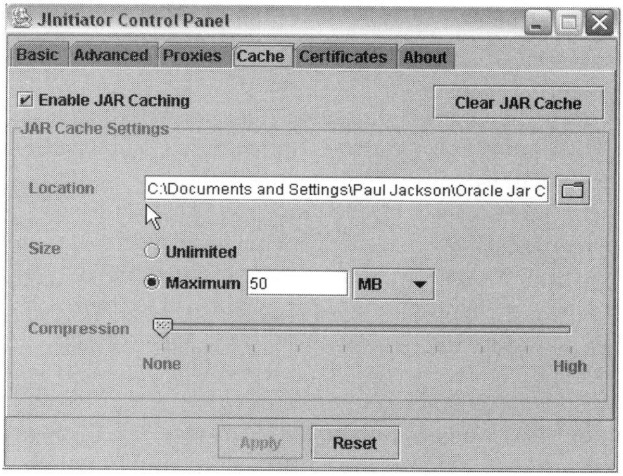

Figure 3-8. *Clearing the JAR Cache*

From this screen, you can also alter the location where the cache is stored and the default size of the cache. This can be useful if there are client issues such as the user not having write permission to the directory where the cache is stored.

Using the Java Console

Java console display settings can be altered using the JInitiator Control Panel. This program may be started from Start ➤ Control Panel menu option on the client PC. There should be a JInitiator icon for each version installed on the computer. Select the appropriate icon to start the program's control panel.

For troubleshooting purposes there is a Show Java Console checkbox on the Basic tab of this control panel. Select this option and click the Apply button to allow for the Java console to be displayed on startup. This will provide the client with some useful troubleshooting information.

■**Tip** If clearing the JInitiator cache and monitoring the Java console do not provide resolution to client Forms issues, it may be necessary to reinstall the JInitiator.

Monitoring and Troubleshooting Best Practices

When it comes to monitoring the Oracle E-Business Suite, the best advice is to be proactive. It is much easier to react to issues before they result in serious problems or outages than to wait for problems to arise.

The key to proactive monitoring is to understand how Oracle Applications is used in your environment. Without knowing what is normal behavior, it is difficult to capture the unexpected. Gain an understanding of the day-to-day activities for your environment, and monitor for exceptions to these trends. As your environment and system change, modify your proactive monitoring to fit new trends.

The best tool for troubleshooting your environment and systems is an understanding of the underlying configuration and how the Oracle E-Business Suite works. Without detailed knowledge of the configuration and functionality, it is difficult to gauge where to begin looking for solutions. Do not be a passive DBA: strive to be an active DBA. Learn the components of the application so that you are empowered to respond quickly when it is broken.

CHAPTER 4

■ ■ ■

Performance Tuning

This chapter will focus on performance tuning techniques for many of the components of the Oracle E-Business Suite. In the course of reading this chapter, you will become familiar with various tools that will enable you to diagnose and fix performance degradation problems.

The two main sections of this chapter focus on the process and tools for performance tuning:

- **Performance tuning process**: The Applications DBA must identify and document the cause of performance degradation, and then develop an action plan for implementing a solution. This section will outline the steps in this process.

- **Tools for resolving performance issues**: This section will discuss several tools that can be used to tune the database and the server and provide tips for tuning Forms, Apache, JServ, and Concurrent Manager. Information for client tuning, generating and analyzing trace files, and some of the new features of Oracle10*g* for SQL statement tuning, will also be covered.

There are numerous books dedicated to the subject of performance tuning. This chapter is not meant to provide intricate details for in-depth performance tuning; however, it will provide an overview of the information required for identifying and resolving performance issues.

■Note Tuning may also be performed on SQL statements and the networking and I/O components of Oracle Applications; however, an extensive discussion of these sorts of tuning is beyond the scope of this guide.

Performance Tuning Process

Performance issues may occur on any of the tiers, infrastructure, or modules that make up the Oracle Applications environment. Because of the complexity of the application, it is necessary to gather information from the user community to determine which component of the application is experiencing the degradation in performance. This section provides you with a method for identifying and documenting performance issues and their resolution.

The first phase is to identify the cause of the degradation by collecting information to help you understand the underlying issue. The second phase is to develop an action plan in order to provide resolution.

Identifying Performance Issues

Traditional methodologies for performance tuning begin with tuning the application code and SQL. Since Oracle E-Business Suite is a packaged application, however, the first step in the traditional methodology is often difficult to implement. There are times when code performs so poorly that assistance from Oracle Support and Development is required to fix the underlying code. This situation will usually surface as a requirement while the Oracle Applications DBA works to identify the underlying performance issue.

To begin resolving performance problems, it is imperative that the nature of the degradation is understood. The strategy presented here for diagnosing the cause of performance degradation starts with general questions and proceeds to questions specific to different pieces of the application: the client tier, the network, a module of the application, and the entire application. It is advisable to document performance issues and the answers to these questions in order to facilitate resolution to the problem.

The Applications DBA may pose the following questions in order to collect the required information. If the answer to a question is no, proceed to the next question.

Question: Can the performance issue be systematically reproduced?

If the answer is yes: Document the process. Proceed to next question.

Question: Is the performance issue observed in only one instance?

If the answer is yes: Determine the difference between the instance where it performs poorly versus the instance where performance is normal. It is possible that the difference is a configuration parameter or a recently applied patch.

Question: Are all users of the application that are experiencing the performance degradation located within the same network segment?

If the answer is yes: The performance issue could be a networking issue. Suggest testing the module on a PC that is located on a different segment of the network. It may be necessary to involve the networking team to capture sniffer tracing on the network segment that is suspected to be performing poorly and to assist in identifying the cause of the underlying network performance problems.

Question: Is the performance degradation limited to a particular window of time?

If the answer is yes: The performance issue could be the result of a scheduled job on the database or server. This job may be causing resource contention. Check all scheduled activity at the application, database, and server level. Monitor the database and server during the time period of performance issues for high resource processes. If a resource-intensive job is found, reschedule it for a better time or acquire more resources to support the required processing.

Question: Is the entire application experiencing performance degradation?

If the answer is yes: Begin monitoring the database and server to identify the underlying performance issue. Tools for monitoring database and server performance are described later in this chapter. Additional methods for troubleshooting are outlined in Chapter 3 of this guide.

Question: Is the performance degradation limited to one module?

If the answer is yes: Ask the user community to provide the name of the module that is performing poorly. Then proceed to work with the user community to open an SR and generate a user trace to provide to Oracle Support. Additional details regarding generating trace files are provided later in this chapter.

Question: Is the performance degradation limited to one user?

If the answer is yes: If only one user is experiencing performance degradation, the degradation is most likely isolated to the client. Suggest that the user experiencing the performance issue try the task on a different workstation. If the user successfully executes the application from a different PC, additional monitoring needs to take place on the user's workstation. It is possible that additional memory or CPU resources are required, or operating system or browser patching is required. Additional tips for diagnosing client issues are discussed later in this chapter.

This list of questions may be enhanced and revised to suit your environment. Update the questions regularly, and keep them in a central location. Be certain that the people providing the first line of support for Oracle Applications are familiar with the questions developed by your organization. If these questions have already been addressed when performance issues are brought to the Applications DBA, the time required to resolve the problem can be reduced.

Additional information can be found in MetaLink Note 69565.1, titled "A Holistic Approach to Performance Tuning Oracle Applications Systems." Using this note and the preceding sample questions, you may begin to develop your own template for performance tuning.

Developing an Action Plan

When a performance problem is reported, the Applications DBA should be able to respond with an action plan for attempting to resolve the issue. Once the issue has been narrowed down to a possible cause, steps for resolving the issue should be outlined. Next, a more detailed tuning effort should take place, focusing on the possible source of problem. The tools discussed in the following section will assist you in determining the steps required for a more detailed tuning effort.

After a resolution to the problem has been identified, update the action plan with the steps taken to resolve the issue. This information can be provided to management and the user community for feedback during the tuning process. This document also becomes a tool for future tuning efforts. If the same problem is encountered again, a potential solution has already been documented.

Tools for Resolving Performance Issues

Tools and methods for identifying and resolving performance issues may be categorized at the database, server, application tier, and user levels. The Applications DBA will need to be familiar with all of these tools. The tools available will vary, depending upon the versions of the database and application installed.

The following topics will be discussed in this section:

- **Database tuning**: Tools for tuning the Oracle9*i* and Oracle10*g* databases are described in this section. For Oracle9*i*, details for executing and analyzing Statspack reports will be given. For Oracle10*g*, the use of the manageability infrastructure, including Active Session History (ASH), Automatic Workload Repository (AWR), and Automatic Database Diagnostics Monitor (ADDM) will be covered.

- **Server tuning**: This section will discuss using UNIX commands, including `top`, `sar`, `vmstat`, and `ps`, to generate performance-related server data. An overview of how to analyze the server data will also be provided.

- **Application tuning**: This section outlines how to analyze performance issues for the following application tiers: Forms, Apache, JServ, and Concurrent Manager. Included in this section are configuration guidelines for improving performance.

- **User tuning**: The use of the Client System Analyzer, an Oracle Applications tool for assessing the client tier, will be covered, and tips for manually analyzing the client will be included.

- **Trace files**: The process for generating trace files for Forms and Self Service applications will be detailed. Steps for using `tkprof` and `trcanlzr` to analyze trace files will also be covered.

- **Additional performance considerations**: Several application profile settings that affect performance will be outlined.

- **Common performance issues**: Common performance problems will be outlined.

Tuning the Database

The best tools for identifying database performance issues are Statspack, provided with Oracle9*i*, or Automatic Workload Repository (AWR), provided with Oracle10*g*. It is possible to perform tuning tasks by querying the Oracle database dictionary, which contains performance-related data, but such tasks are beyond the scope of this guide. We will rely on using the standard Oracle tools, such as Statspack, Automatic Workload Repository, and Automatic Database Diagnostic Monitoring for collecting system performance data. Tool availability is dependent upon the version of the database.

Using Statspack for Oracle9*i*

Statspack is an Oracle-provided utility comprising PL/SQL code and scripts that are used for collecting and storing performance data. The perfstat user owns the Statspack database objects, including packages and tables. Please review information specific to your database version for installation of the Statspack utility.

■**Tip** When defining the perfstat user, be sure to set the default tablespace to a tablespace other than SYSTEM, such as the TOOLS tablespace. Also, set the temporary tablespace for the perfstat user to a temporary tablespace defined in the database instance, such as TEMP.

When using Oracle Applications, additional scripts are available to enhance the Statspack utility. MetaLink Note 153507.1 describes 11*i* Statspack specifics in detail. One additional script of interest, spmodfn.sql, may be executed to include the source module name of queries in the output of a Statspack report.

Once Statspack has been installed, a snapshot of the database may be taken, to collect performance information. Two snapshots are required to generate a performance collection window. Reports can then be generated to analyze database performance for the time period between two snapshots.

■**Tip** When generating snapshot reports, the two snapshots should not include a period when the database was shut down; if it does, the report will be invalid.

The SQL*Plus command in the following example may be executed as the perfstat user to obtain a default snapshot:

```
sql>exec statspack.snapshot
```

Some parameters for thresholds should be changed from their default when executing Statspack snapshots for Oracle Applications. These are listed in Table 4-1.

Table 4-1. *Statspack Thresholds and Descriptions*

Parameter Name	Description
i_snap_level	Snapshot level; level 0 is the most general collection, and 10 is the most detailed
i_executioins_th	SQL threshold; number of times the statement was executed
i_parse_calls_th	SQL threshold; number of parse calls the statement made
i_disk_reads_th	SQL threshold; number of disk reads the statement made
i_buffer_gets_th	SQL threshold; number of buffer gets the statement made
i_sharable_mem_th	SQL threshold; amount of memory required to execute the statement
i_version_count_th	SQL threshold; number of versions (children cursors) used by the statement
i_all_init	When set to TRUE, Statspack will capture all non-default Oracle initialization parameters

The following example shows the recommended thresholds for snapshots taken on Oracle Applications:

```
sql>exec statspack.snapshot ( -
>i_snap_level        =>    6, -
>i_executions_th     =>    1000, -
>i_parse_calls_th    =>    1000, -
>i_disk_reads_th     =>    10000, -
>i_buffer_gets_th    =>    100000, -
>i_sharable_mem_th   =>    1048576, -
>i_version_count_th  =>    20, -
>i_all_init          =>    'TRUE' -
>)
```

■**Tip** The timed_statistics database initialization parameter must be set to TRUE in order to use Statspack.

It is advisable to collect snapshots during periods of normal activity in the system to provide a baseline of comparison for snapshots that are taken during periods when performance degradation is being experienced. In order to compare information, snapshots should be of the same duration and be executed during the same level and type of activity. Enterprise Manager (EM), dbms_jobs, or crontab may be used to schedule snapshots on a regular basis. The use of these methods for scheduling activities will be described in Chapter 6 of this guide. The spauto.sql script in the $ORACLE_HOME/rdbms/admin directory will schedule snapshots to execute every hour.

▓Tip Executing a snapshot at the start and end of a payroll run is a good example of when regularly scheduled snapshots should be scheduled.

Once snapshots have been captured, the sprepins.sql script should be executed as the perfstat user in order to generate the performance report. The database ID and beginning and ending snapshot numbers are required input for the sprepins.sql report to be generated. The following example shows the command to generate a Statspack report:

```
sql>@$ORACLE_HOME/rdbms/admin/sprepins.sql
```

```
Instances in this Statspack schema
~~~~~~~~~~~~~~~~~~~~~~~~~~~~~~~~~~~~

  DB Id    Inst Num DB Name     Instance     Host
----------- -------- ------------ ------------ ------------
3015003723        1 VIS          VIS          vis1

Enter value for dbid:
```

After entering the DB ID and instance number, the script will display a list of available snapshot IDs. The script will prompt for a beginning and an ending snapshot ID to be used for the report.

Analyzing Oracle9*i* Statspack Reports

Once the database performance data has been generated with Statspack, the Applications DBA will need to review the report. The report will contain much useful information, such as instance efficiency percentages, top timed events, and top SQL, ordered by several criteria, such as physical reads, logical reads, and executions, among others. An example of a Statspack report is shown in Figure 4-1.

```
DB Name          DB Id    Instance     Inst Num Release      Cluster Host
-----------  -----------  -----------  -------- -----------  ------- ------------
VIS          1236112810   VIS              1    9.2.0.6.0    NO      hostname

                Snap Id    Snap Time       Sessions Curs/Sess Comment
                -------  ------------------ -------- --------- -------------------
Begin Snap:         10  13-Oct-06 10:00:04     410     70.8
  End Snap:         11  13-Oct-06 11:00:04     593     76.2
  Elapsed:                    60.00 (mins)
...

Instance Efficiency Percentages (Target 100%)
~~~~~~~~~~~~~~~~~~~~~~~~~~~~~~~~~~~~~~~~~~~~~~~~~
                    Buffer Nowait %:     99.99      Redo NoWait %:   100.00
                       Buffer Hit  %:    95.09   In-memory Sort %:   100.00
                      Library Hit  %:    99.92        Soft Parse %:    98.18
                 Execute to Parse %:     96.10        Latch Hit %:     99.08
        Parse CPU to Parse Elapsd %:     72.15    % Non-Parse CPU:     93.49

Top 5 Timed Events
~~~~~~~~~~~~~~~~~~~                                                   % Total
Event                                           Waits     Time (s) Ela Time
-------------------------------------------- ------------ --------- --------
db file scattered read                         6,931,234   808,206    59.11
db file sequential read                          646,861   466,845    34.14
CPU time                                          53,209     3.17
library cache lock                             1,673,310    22,580     1.65
enqueue                                        1,830,410    11,509      .84
...

SQL ordered by Gets for DB: VIS    Instance: VIS    Snaps: 10 -11
-> End Buffer Gets Threshold:   100000
-> Note that resources reported for PL/SQL includes the resources used by
   all SQL statements called within the PL/SQL code. As individual SQL
   statements are also reported, it is possible and valid for the summed
   total % to exceed 100

                                               CPU      Elapsd
 Buffer Gets     Executions  Gets per Exec  %Total Time (s)  Time (s) Hash Value
--------------- ------------  -------------  ------ --------  --------- ----------
   206,218,885            2   103,109,442.5     8.1  1817.02   2135.90 1345408540
Module: MODULE_NAME
SELECT  * FROM sales

   173,585,391        2,064      84,10|1.4     6.8  1318.22   1754.78  715500204
Module: MODULE_NAME
SELECT  * FROM emp
...
```

Figure 4-1. *Sample Statspack report*

The top wait or timed events listed in the report identify the events that might require tuning. The "SQL Ordered By" sections of the report can help identify SQL statements that require tuning or that are CPU intensive. This data is necessary for finding the root cause of performance issues.

The key to improving performance is to spend time tuning items that will result in the biggest improvement. Little will be gained by spending an inordinate amount of time tuning an event that is a minor consumer of system resources. Spend time focusing on the largest resource consumers.

For example, if the performance data indicates that "db file scattered read" is by far the biggest wait event, the Applications DBA needs to look for the cause of this problem. This wait event can be caused by an excessive number of full table scan queries. The full table scans could be the result of bad database statistics causing the optimizer to build inefficient execution plans, or poorly written queries that are not taking advantage of existing indexes. Occasionally such a problem may be resolved by creating an additional index, but be aware that creating an index results in the additional cost of extra storage space as well as overhead for Data Manipulation Language (DML) statements against the underlying table.

In addition to reviewing the top wait events, also review the top SQL statements in the categories of logical reads, physical reads, and number of executions. These investigations may reveal SQL statements that require tuning. With a packaged application such as Oracle E-Business Suite, it may not be possible to rewrite problem queries, and in extreme situations it may be necessary to open an SR with Oracle to resolve the performance problems.

By including the module name in the Statspack report, the Applications DBA may be able to search MetaLink for information about that module's SQL performance to identify known performance issues. Ensure that the module in question is patched with the highest level of code possible.

Finally, when reviewing the performance data, look for any problems with the memory sizing. Oracle Applications can require large shared pool, buffer cache, and PGA aggregate settings. A low buffer cache hit ratio may be resolved by increasing the buffer cache size. However, be sure to investigate all scenarios before adding memory. It does the system no good to increase memory size when the root problem is outdated database statistics or skewed buffer hit ratios resulting from Concurrent Manager or workflow data not being properly purged from the system.

Using Active Session History with Oracle10*g*

A key element of Oracle10*g*'s manageability infrastructure is Active Session History (ASH). Oracle collects information every second on active database sessions and stores this information in memory within the System Global Area (SGA). By collecting this data, the Automatic Database Diagnostics Monitor (ADDM) process will be able to better identify issues related to data access by sessions. The MMNL background process is responsible for writing session data to memory. This should enable performance data to be collected with minimal overhead to the system. The MMNL process will write the data from memory into tables every hour.

ASH data can be accessed through the V$ACTIVE_SESSION_HISTORY view for manual analysis. This view contains information about the database user, the module being run, SQL execution plans, wait events, CPU time used, and database objects being accessed. Given the frequency of samples from Oracle, this view will contain current data, and it makes ASH useful for near real-time analysis of your system. To view information collected by ASH for a specific duration, run the ashrpt.sql script in the $ORACLE_HOME/rdbms/admin directory on the Database Node.

In addition to performing online analysis, the contents of the ASH buffer may be downloaded to a trace file. The process for doing this utilizes the

ASHDUMP event:

`sql>alter session set events 'immediate trace name ashdump level 10';`

This command will create a trace file in the database's udump directory. The file created will be a comma-separated text file containing a structure similar to the V$ACTIVE_SESSION_HISTORY view. For analysis, this file may be loaded into the database using the SQL Loader utility. Utilizing ASHDUMP allows for offline analysis, which can be useful for analyzing the data from a hung system. Also, the dump file can be imported into a different system, in case the target system becomes unavailable.

Using Automatic Workload Repository with Oracle10*g*

In Oracle10g, snapshots no longer need to be executed manually, as with Statspack. The Automatic Workload Repository (AWR) collects performance data automatically. The data collection is done with minimal overhead by utilizing a new background process called Manageability Monitor (MMON), which is responsible for taking the snapshots of database performance statistics. Building this sort of performance diagnostic information into the database is part of Oracle's new manageability infrastructure. AWR is not just a replacement of Statspack—additional information is gathered by AWR, such as operating system statistics, which can be seen in the V$OSSTAT view.

The default collection method used by MMON is to take snapshots every 60 minutes. This data is stored for seven days before it is automatically purged from the system. Rather than using a perfstat user and a TOOLS tablespace, this data is stored in the SYS schema within the SYSAUX tablespace. Over 100 tables are created to store the AWR data, which can be accessed using the DBA_HIST_% views. Some of the more common views are listed in Table 4-2.

Table 4-2. *Common AWR Views*

View name	Description
DBA_HIST_BASELINE	Information on the AWR baselines
DBA_HIST_DATABASE_INSTANCE	Information on the database and instance
DBA_HIST_SNAPSHOT	Information on AWR snapshots
DBA_HIST_SQL_PLAN	Information on SQL execution plans
DBA_HIST_WR_CONTROL	Information on the parameters set for AWR

Oracle EM provides a graphical interface for managing AWR. Using EM, the Applications DBA can easily manage the AWR settings and generate reports.

The management of AWR may also be performed using the DBMS_WORKLOAD_REPOSITORY package. For example, to change the frequency of snapshots from one hour to two hours, and data retention from seven days to ten days, execute the following command using numbers of minutes for the two parameters:

```
sql>exec dbms_workload_repository.modify_snapshot_settings ( -
>interval => 120, -
>retention => 14400)
```

To manually create a snapshot when the snapshot interval is not sufficient, use the following procedure:

```
sql>exec dbms_workload_repository.create_snapshot()
```

Within AWR it is possible to create a baseline of snapshots, and in EM this feature is called Preserved Snapshot Sets. This baseline may be created from snapshots taken during periods of normal database activity. If problems occur at a later date, a new baseline may be created, and these two baselines can be compared to identify performance problems. To create a baseline from snapshot_id 1 and snapshot_id 2, use the following command:

```
sql>exec dbms_workload_repository.create_baseline( -
>start_snap_id => 1, -
>end_snap_id => 2, -
>baseline_name => 'Test')
```

The performance report is generated by running the awrrpt.sql script. This script requires two snapshots covering the time when the performance issue was experienced as input. Here is an example of executing the AWR performance report:

```
sql>@$ORACLE_HOME/rdbms/admin/awrrpt.sql
```

The report may be manually analyzed using the same approach as for analyzing Statspack reports. With Oracle10g, the Automatic Database Diagnostic Monitoring (ADDM) can automatically analyze AWR information. The features of this tool are explained in the next section.

Using Automatic Database Diagnostic Monitoring with Oracle 10*g*

The goal of the manageability infrastructure is to provide a self-monitoring and self-tuning database. This feature should free the DBA from mundane tasks and allow more time for providing strategic direction. Rather than recommending the DBA manually analyze AWR and ASH data, Oracle provides the Automatic Database Diagnostic Monitor (ADDM) to automatically analyze the data collected by the monitoring tools. By following a set of tuning rules developed by Oracle experts, this program will create recommendations that will reduce overall time spent in database calls.

The ADDM analysis will list areas for improvement in its reports that are not necessarily critical. Keep in mind that the goal of tuning is to seek the areas where you can make the biggest improvement.

■**Tip** Be careful when using any automatic analysis tool. The recommendations provided by the tool may not be appropriate for your system. Before implementing any recommendation from such a tool, be sure that you understand the reasoning for the change. Thoroughly test any such change before promoting the change to your production system.

Like AWR and ASH, EM provides a rich, graphical interface to ADDM. EM's interface to these tools provides the easiest method of interaction. However, you may still perform analysis and build reports manually as a database user with the ADVISOR privilege by using the Oracle-provided DBMS_ADVISOR package. The $ORACLE_HOME/rdbms/admin/addmrpt.sql script will generate an ADDM report.

The method of executing this script is very similar to generating a Statspack report. You will be prompted for a beginning and ending AWR snapshot to use for the analysis. If the database has been restarted during the time between the two snapshots, the analysis provided by ADDM will be invalid.

■**Note** In order for ADDM to function, the STATISTICS_LEVEL initialization parameter must be set to either TYPICAL or ALL. A setting of BASIC will disable ADDM. Oracle recommends only setting this parameter to ALL when performing diagnostics on the system.

Information related to ADDM may be accessed in the DBA_ADVISOR_% views. Some of the more important views are listed in Table 4-3.

Table 4-3. *Common ADDM Views*

View Name	Description
DBA_ADVISOR_FINDINGS	Information on the findings of ADDM
DBA_ADVISOR_LOG	Information on the current state of all tasks in the database
DBA_ADVISOR_RATIONALE	Information on the rationale for all recommendations by ADDM
DBA_ADVISOR_RECOMMENDATIONS	Information on the recommendations for all diagnostic tasks
DBA_ADVISOR_TASKS	Information on the existing tasks in the database

Tuning the Server

All of the database tuning in the world cannot eliminate performance issues if the underlying problem is at the server level. Standard UNIX commands can be used to monitor server CPU and memory consumption. Some of the commands vary depending upon the flavor of UNIX used, so consult documentation specific to your operating system for more detail. All of the commands discussed in this section have many parameters and options associated with them; therefore, an overview of how to use the commands will be provided.

Using top

The UNIX top command provides an overview of CPU and memory utilization. The statistics are refreshed every few seconds to provide near real-time data. Statistics for CPU, memory, and swap space for the top command are shown in Tables 4-4 through 4-6.

Table 4-4. *CPU States as Displayed by* top

Column	Description
User	Percentage of CPU utilized by user
System	Percentage of CPU utilized by the server
Idle	Percentage of CPU idle time

Table 4-5. *Memory as Displayed by* top

Column	Description
Av	Available memory
Used	Used memory
Free	Free memory

Table 4-6. *Swap as Displayed by* top

Column	Description
Av	Available swap space
Used	Used swap space
Free	Free swap space

Upon executing top, the CPU, memory, and swap statistics are displayed, followed by a list of active system processes. The process information displayed is very similar to what is displayed by the ps command, which will be described shortly in the "Using ps" section. To exit top, press **q**. An example of executing top is displayed in Figure 4-2.

```
  2:55pm  up 54 days,   6:21,   4 users,   load average: 0.74, 1.40, 1.55
467 processes: 461 sleeping, 6 running, 0 zombie, 0 stopped
CPU states:   3.3% user,   0.9% system,   0.0% nice,  95.6% idle
Mem:   2059384K av, 1919828K used,   139556K free,      33672K shrd,    206940K buff
Swap: 2096440K av,   260928K used, 1835512K free                        770256K cached

  PID USER     PRI  NI  SIZE   RSS  SHARE STAT %CPU %MEM   TIME COMMAND
13241 oracle    16   0  1548  1548   828 R    1.1  0.0   0:00 top
 1357 root      15   0 15044  1816  1172 S    0.1  0.0  28:57 X
    1 root      15   0   504   456   440 S    0.0  0.0   0:04 init
    2 root      15   0     0     0     0 SW   0.0  0.0   0:00 keventd
    3 root      34  19     0     0     0 SWN  0.0  0.0   0:38 ksoftirqd_CPU0
    4 root      15   0     0     0     0 RW   0.0  0.0   3:06 kswapd
    5 root      15   0     0     0     0 SW   0.0  0.0   0:00 kreclaimd
    6 root      15   0     0     0     0 SW   0.0  0.0   0:35 bdflush
    7 root      15   0     0     0     0 SW   0.0  0.0   0:08 kupdated
    8 root      25   0     0     0     0 SW   0.0  0.0   0:00 mdrecoveryd
   16 root      15   0     0     0     0 SW   0.0  0.0   0:39 kjournald
  101 root      16   0     0     0     0 SW   0.0  0.0   0:00 khubd
  193 root      15   0     0     0     0 SW   0.0  0.0   0:00 kjournald
  194 root      15   0     0     0     0 SW   0.0  0.0   0:19 kjournald
  732 root      15   0   584   564   564 S    0.0  0.0   0:02 syslogd
  737 root      15   0  1136   436   436 S    0.0  0.0   0:00 klogd
  757 rpc       15   0   620   600   596 S    0.0  0.0   0:11 portmap
```

Figure 4-2. *Execution of* top

Using sar

System Activity Reporter (sar) has many different parameters that can be used. CPU utilization can be shown with the -u switch, for example, and memory swapping can be shown with the -w switch.

The sar command requires two arguments, the first being the time interval between samples, and the second being the number of samples to take. Table 4-7 lists relevant columns and descriptions of the data displayed by executing sar -u to capture CPU utilization.

Table 4-7. *Columns and Descriptions for the* sar -u *Command*

Column	Description
%user	Percentage of system utilized by users
%system	Percentage of system utilized by the OS
%iowait	Percentage waiting on I/O
%idle	Percentage of server that is idle

Figure 4-3 shows the output of the sar -u command, displaying CPU utilization with five samples in 10-second intervals.

```
$ sar -u 10 5

02:57:46 PM    CPU    %user    %nice    %system    %iowait    %idle
02:57:56 PM    all     2.50     0.00      1.20       0.00      96.30
02:58:06 PM    all     1.70     0.00      1.70       0.00      96.60
02:58:16 PM    all     1.20     0.40      2.10       0.00      96.30
02:58:26 PM    all     2.20     0.00      1.40       0.00      96.40
02:58:36 PM    all     2.30     0.00      1.40       0.00      96.30
Average:       all     1.98     0.08      1.56       0.00      96.38
```

Figure 4-3. *Executing* sar -u

Table 4-8 lists relevant columns and descriptions of the data displayed by executing sar -r to capture memory utilization.

Table 4-8. *Statistics Displayed by the* sar -r *Command*

Column	Description
kbmemfree	Free memory in KB
kbmemused	Memory used in KB
%memused	Percentage of memory used
kbswpfree	Free swap space in KB
kbswpused	Used swap space in KB
%swpused	Percentage of used swap space

Figure 4-4 shows the output of the sar -r command, displaying server data for six samples with 5-second intervals between each sample.

```
$ sar -r 5 6
09:44:55 AM  kbmemfree  kbmemused  %memused  kbbuffers  kbcached  kbswpfree  kbswpused  %swpused  kbswpcad
09:45:00 AM     464336    1595048     77.45     201672     686192    1722212     374228     17.85     156956
09:45:05 AM     464336    1595048     77.45     201672     686192    1722212     374228     17.85     156956
09:45:10 AM     464336    1595048     77.45     201672     686192    1722212     374228     17.85     156956
09:45:15 AM     464336    1595048     77.45     201672     686196    1722212     374228     17.85     156956
09:45:20 AM     464336    1595048     77.45     201672     686196    1722212     374228     17.85     156956
09:45:25 AM     464336    1595048     77.45     201672     686196    1722212     374228     17.85     156956
Average:        464336    1595048     77.45     201672     686194    1722212     374228     17.85     156956
```

Figure 4-4. *Execution of* sar -r

Using vmstat

Another command that can be used to display UNIX performance statistics is vmstat. Common statistics displayed by vmstat are arranged in the categories shown in Table 4-9.

Table 4-9. *Categories for the* vmstat *Command*

Category	Description
procs	Information about processes
memory	Information about virtual and real memory
wwap	Information about page faults and paging activity
io	Information about I/O
system	Information about system interrupts and switches
cpu	Information about percentage of CPU time

Additional details for key vmstat columns in the different categories are shown in Table 4-10.

Table 4-10. *Key* vmstat *Statistics*

Column	Description
r	Run queue
free	Amount of idle memory (KB)
si	Amount of memory swapped in from disk (KB/s)
so	Amount of memory swapped to disk (KB/s)
bi	Blocks sent to a device
bo	Blocks received from a device

Continued

Table 4-10. *Continued*

Column	Description
us	User time
sy	System time
id	Idle time

Executing vmstat without any options results in statistics being displayed since the last reboot, as shown in Figure 4-5.

```
$ vmstat

   procs                      memory      swap          io     system        cpu
 r  b  w   swpd   free   buff  cache  si  so    bi   bo   in   cs  us sy id
 1  0  0 260928 139556 206940 770304   0   0     3    0    4    3   9  3  6
```

Figure 4-5. *Server statistics displayed by* vmstat

The example of vmstat in Figure 4-6 displays five summaries at 3-second intervals, the first summary being the summary since boot up.

```
$ vmstat 3 5

   procs                      memory      swap          io     system         cpu
 r  b  w   swpd   free   buff  cache  si  so    bi   bo    in   cs  us sy id
 0  0  0 260928 139556 206940 770324   0   0     3    0   | 4    3   9  3  6
14  0  0 260928 139556 206940 770324   0   0     0   51  166 1035   4  3 94
 9  0  0 260928 139556 206940 770324   0   0     0   49  143 1003   1  1 98
 8  0  0 260928 139556 206940 770324   0   0     0    0  141 1031   4  2 94
 9  0  0 260928 139556 206940 770324   0   0     0   55  163 1024   5  3 92
```

Figure 4-6. *Summary of server statistics displayed by* vmstat 3 5

Using ps

The UNIX ps command is used to display active processes. This command can be sorted by any of the columns that are displayed by it. Sorting by the sixth column, the CPU column, is demonstrated in Figure 4-7. The columns displayed in the output in Figure 4-7 are process, process ID, parent process ID, CPU utilization of process, total execution time, controlling workstation, login time, process owner.

```
$ps -ef |sort +6|tail

oracle 2547924 1 0 03:50:32 - 0:54 VIS
oracle 2683076 1 0 10:42:16 - 1:31 VIS
oracle 6840400 1 10 10:42:17 - 1:31 VIS
oracle 6369314 1 1 10:42:17 - 1:32 VIS
oracle 6991876 1 0 10:42:16 - 1:33 VIS
oracle 3465274 1 0 10:42:17 - 1:33 VIS
oracle 1720334 1 0 11:28:06 - 1:33 VIS
oracle 4493540 1 17 16:44:05 - 1:34 VIS
```

Figure 4-7. *Sorting processes by CPU with the* ps *command*

Analyzing Server Performance Data

By using any of the UNIX commands described in the previous sections, key performance statistics for the server can be gathered. CPU usage, memory usage, and resource-intensive processes should be furthered analyzed.

If the CPU is displaying small amounts of idle time, it is possible that Oracle processes are experiencing CPU contention. If CPU consumption cannot be associated with one process but rather is the sum of many processes, additional CPU resources may be required. Within vmstat, the number displayed for the run queue should be less than the total number of CPUs on the server.

If the top CPU consumer is an Oracle process, you should identify the source of the process. If it is on the application server, determine if it is a Forms, iAS, or Concurrent Manager process. Review the log files for errors or use some of the monitoring tools previously discussed to determine the cause of the high activity. Sometimes it may be necessary to bounce the Forms or Apache Server or kill the process at the operating system level to remove a process that is spinning out of control. If the process is on the database server, drill down into the underlying activity in the database for the session that matches the UNIX process ID. This may be accomplished with EM or by executing queries in the database. Use Statspack or AWR, or generate user traces to determine whether the database process needs to be tuned in order to reduce CPU utilization.

Memory swapping occurs if real memory is exhausted and its contents need to be swapped to disk. If there is a high amount of memory swapping, it is likely that Oracle is experiencing memory contention. It might be possible to decrease the amount of memory being consumed by the SGA or iAS, but often memory contention is resolved by purchasing additional RAM for the server.

Tuning the Application Tier

Common application components that require performance-tuning attention include Forms, Apache Server, JServ, and Concurrent Manager.

Forms Tuning

Forms sessions run on the server as f60webmx processes. You can retrieve a listing of the Forms processes on the server for the VIS instance by executing the following command:

```
$ps -ef | grep f60webmx | grep VIS
```

If an f60webmx process is one of the top processes on a server, as determined by top, sar, or ps, you should try to link the Forms process to a database session. This can be done by viewing active Forms sessions in OAM as outlined in Chapter 3 of this guide. If there seems to be no valid reason for this session to be among the top sessions, then it might be necessary to kill the session or bounce the Forms server.

Forms performance issues may arise when dead connections persist on the server, consuming server resources. Enabling Forms dead-client detection by setting the FORMS60_TIMEOUT parameter can eliminate dead connections. The value specified for the parameter is in minutes.

Another means of tuning Forms processes is to enable the Forms abnormal termination handler by enabling the FORMS60_CATCHTERM parameter. Setting FORMS60_CATCHTERM to 1 will cause Forms errors to dump output to the FORMS60_TRACE_PATH directory.

Both the FORMS60_TIMEOUT and FORMS60_CATCHTERM parameters can be set by modifying the context file and then running autoconfig or by exporting them as environment variables and restarting the Forms server.

Key context file parameters for Forms tuning are shown in Table 4-11.

Table 4-11. *Parameters for Forms Tuning Sessions*

Context File Parameter	Environment Variable	Recommended Value
s_f60time	FORMS60_TIMEOUT	10
s_f60catchterm	FORMS60_CATCHTERM	unset or 1

Users of the Oracle E-Business Suite may also want the ability to cancel a Forms query. This may be achieved by setting the FND: Enable Cancel Query profile option to Yes at the site, application, responsibility, or user level. If you do not enable this profile option, the only method for canceling the query is to kill the Forms session. When this profile option is enabled, a cancel query dialog box will appear in order for the user to cancel the query. Review MetaLink Note 138159.1 for additional requirements, such as Forms patch level.

While this seems like a good feature to offer your users, it comes at the expense of increasing client, middle-tier, and database CPU usage. Be careful when enabling this feature. Since it can be controlled down to the user level, it is recommended that you limit this option to certain users. If you decide to enable cancel query, the parameters shown in Table 4-12 may be used to tune its effects.

Table 4-12. *Environment Variables Used to Tune the Cancel Query Feature*

Environment Variable	Value	Description
FORMS60_LOV_INITIAL	1000–32000	Number of milliseconds until the cancel query button appears to the user.
FORMS60_LOV_MINIMUM	1000–32000	Value in milliseconds between polling of the client from the middle tier to check whether the query cancel dialog box should be popped. Recommended values are 1000–5000
FORMS60_LOV_WEIGHT	0–32000	Value used to assist in determining network latency, in order to adjust the polling period.

The FORMS60_LOV_INITIAL environment variable can assist in reducing network traffic. Set it close to the maximum value in order to reduce network traffic. The FORMS60_LOV_MINIMUM environment variable specifies how frequently polling occurs. The more frequent the polling, the more quickly the query will be cancelled. The FORMS60_LOV_WEIGHT environment variable uses an equation to determine network latency in order to reduce the number of round trips.

The FORMS60_LOV_INITIAL, FORMS60_LOV_MINIMUM, and FORMS60_LOV_WEIGHT environment variables must be set in the $APPL_TOP/<SID>.env environment file, or in the formservlet.ini file if you are using the Forms Servlet Listener. The following example shows the settings of the values in the $APPL_TOP/<SID>.env environment file:

```
export FORMS60_LOV_INITIAL=32000
export FORMS60_LOV_MINIMUM=5000
export FORMS60_LOV_WEIGHT=0
```

Once the variables have been set, the environment should be sourced and the Forms Server bounced. Be certain to test the effects of setting these parameters before promoting them to your production environment. In order to prevent autoconfig from overwriting the values, add them to your context file or review the approach for adding custom values in Chapter 2.

■**Tip** The `MAXBLOCKTIME` value in the `formservlet.properties` file must be larger than the maximum query polling interval. This is only required if you are using the Forms Servlet Listener. The default value is 1000ms. If `MAXBLOCKTIME` is not set greater than the query polling interval, this will result in excessive CPU usage, which will cause performance degradation.

Apache Tuning

The Apache Server runs on the server as `httpd` processes. You may retrieve a listing of the Apache processes on the server for the VIS instance by executing the following:

```
$ps -ef | grep httpd| grep vis
```

When it comes to the Apache Server, be sure to set logging at the lowest level possible. Excessive logging and debugging may result in performance degradation. For standard operations, keep the log levels in the `httpd.conf` file set to `warn`. If the levels are changed for troubleshooting purposes, ensure that the levels are reset before resuming normal usage. The lowest logging levels in the `httpd.conf` file are as follows:

```
LogLevel=warn
SSLLogLevel=warn
```

Caching non-HTML objects will also improve Apache performance. Caching directives are automatically set if you are using autoconfig, or they can be set in either the `httpd.conf` or `apps.conf` file using the following guidelines:

```
#
# enable caching for OA_HTML/cabo/jsLibs
#
<Directory substitute_path_to_OA_HTML/cabo/jsLibs>
ExpiresActive On
ExpiresByType application/x-javascript "access plus 1 year"
ExpiresByType text/javascript "access plus 1 year"
</Directory>
#
# enable caching for OA_HTML/cabo/oajsLibs
#
<Directory substitute_path_to_OA_HTML/cabo/oajsLibs>
ExpiresActive On
```

```
ExpiresByType application/x-javascript "access plus 1 year"
ExpiresByType text/javascript "access plus 1 year"
</Directory>
#
# enable caching for OA_MEDIA
#
<Directory substitute_path_to_OA_MEDIA>
ExpiresActive On
ExpiresByType image/gif "access plus 1 month"
ExpiresByType image/jpeg "access plus 1 month"
</Directory>
```

JServ Tuning

JServ processes are children processes of the httpd Apache process that run on the server. As with the Apache Server, you should set JServ logging to its lowest level in order to minimize the performance degradation that is caused by logging. JServ logging is set in the jserv.properties, jserv.conf, and ssp_init.txt files. To reduce logging, ensure that the JServ configuration files have the following parameter settings:

```
jserv.conf:
ApJServLogLevel warn

jserv.properties:
Log=false
Log.channel.info=false
Log.channel.debug=false
Log.channel.warning=true

ssp_init.txt:
Debug_switch=OFF
```

The FND: View Object Max Fetch Size profile can be set to limit the number of rows an executed query returns to a user in an HTML application. You should set this profile to no greater than 200. If this number is increased, JServ memory can be exhausted. If the value of 200 is not great enough, you should set the profile at the application level for the application that requires the ability to return more rows. This will reduce the overall impact of the parameter.

If the session timeout, set by the session.timeout parameter in the zone.properties file, is greater than 30 minutes, session memory usage may result in performance degradation. Be certain to set the session timeout to the lowest acceptable level for your user community.

This brings us to an integral tuning step for JServ tuning: evaluating the heap memory settings for the JServs in the `jserv.properties` file. Additional details on monitoring the JVM heap size with the AM Pool Monitor are outlined in Chapter 3 of this guide. Improperly tuned memory settings may result in performance problems with web-based applications. If JServ log files or browser sessions report an "out of memory" error, the JVM most likely has hit a memory limitation. If this occurs, you should increase the JVM heap size parameter in the `jserv.properties` file as follows:

```
wrapper.bin.parameters=-mx<new_size>m
```

Another parameter that can be tuned to assist JVM performance is one that controls the automatic reloading of new classes. This feature allows new classes to be used without requiring a restart of the JServ. Turning off this feature will increase performance because the JServs will no longer check for modifications. By default, the `autoreload.classes` parameter is set to `true`. To disable this feature, edit the `zone.properties` file as follows:

```
autoreload.classes=false
```

At times it is necessary to bounce the Apache Server and delete the cache. This may result in performance degradation while the cache is being rebuilt. Upon Apache startup, you can cache frequently used classes by setting the following parameter in the `zone.properties` file:

```
servlets.startup=oracle.apps.fnd.framework.OAStartupServlet
```

JDK releases typically include performance enhancements; therefore, as with other components of the applications tier, upgrading to the latest version of JDK available will help the performance of your Java servlets.

■**Tip** After modifying and testing changes to the configuration files, you should update the context file with the new values so the changes remain permanent for subsequent executions of `adconfig`.

Concurrent Manager Tuning

Performance problems on the applications tier may also arise from contention with resource-intensive Concurrent Manager jobs. The solution for this issue could result in implementing architecture changes, performing regular maintenance on the Concurrent Manager tables, or tuning jobs.

As part of an overall strategy for concurrent processing, multiple Concurrent Managers should be defined to handle long running and short running requests. It may also be necessary to define module-specific Concurrent Managers—for example, a long running Concurrent Manager for GL and a long running Concurrent Manager for AP. Much of this is dependent upon the scheduling requirements for your site.

The Oracle E-Business Suite's predefined Concurrent Manager is called the Standard Manager. The Standard Manager should be reserved for standard Oracle requests. In order to support a large volume of concurrent requests, it may also be necessary to implement Parallel Concurrent Processing by load balancing concurrent requests across multiple nodes.

■**Tip** Schedule as many Concurrent Manager processes as possible during non-peak hours to reduce contention with the daily business processing.

Concurrent Manager performance problems could also result from not purging concurrent request history on a regular basis. Detailed information regarding purging this history is outlined in Chapter 6 of this guide. One symptom of this problem would be a low buffer cache hit ratio in the Statspack report. Keep a minimal amount of Concurrent Manager data in the system. Oracle recommends setting the purge to keep no more than 30 days worth of data online. If your environment generates an excessive amount of concurrent activity, you may consider limiting the history to less than 30 days. The requirements for retaining Concurrent Manager output are environment specific.

If performance problems are related to one particular job, focus on tuning that job. For Oracle-seeded jobs, you should consider opening an SR. If statistics are up to date on the objects being queried by the job, the problem may be a known bug with the concurrent request. Oracle Support should be able to provide guidance for resolving the issue.

If performance problems are associated with a custom job, the Applications DBA and development team should work to tune the job. The user trace and SQL tuning information presented later in this chapter can assist with that tuning effort. A custom Concurrent Manager may be required to processes certain jobs. MetaLink Note 170524.1 provides details for creating a custom Concurrent Manager.

If performance problems are associated with one particular manager, and there appears to be high CPU consumption on the Concurrent Processing Node, the ICM Sleep Time may be set to a value too low for your system. MetaLink Note 178925.1 describes the process of altering the ICM Sleep Time setting.

User Tuning

Inadequate resources on the workstation often cause performance degradation on the client. You should review client recommendations for the version of the application that is running in your company.

Using the Client System Analyzer

If you are running 11.5.10 or OAM.H rollup 1, performance issues on the client can be diagnosed using the Client System Analyzer tool provided by Oracle. The Client System Analyzer is executed from any form by going to the Help ➤ Diagnostics Menu ➤ Client System Analyzer. After selecting these menu options, the Client System Analyzer applet and a compatible Java Virtual Machine (JVM) will be downloaded.

This tool will collect CPU, memory, operating system, and other relevant workstation information. To view the results of the analysis, click the View Results button. The Client System Analyzer is displayed in Figure 4-8.

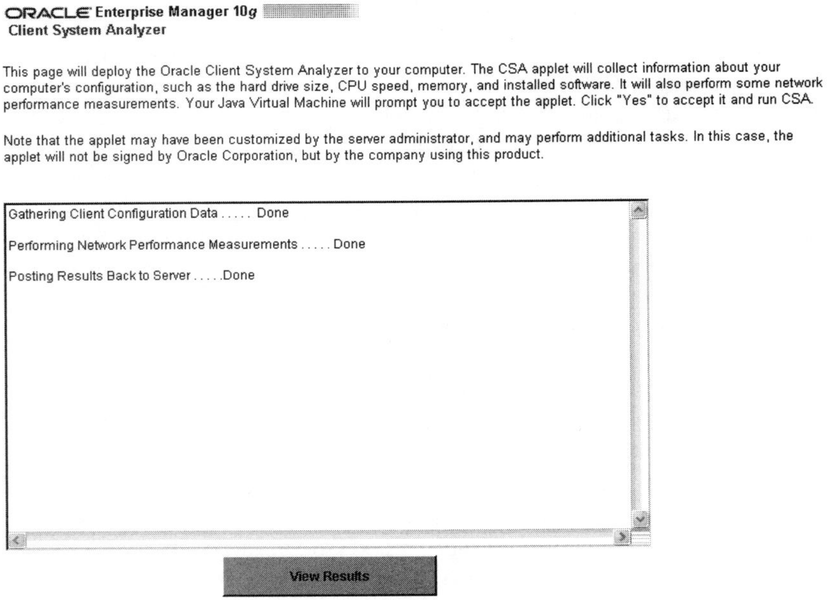

ORACLE Enterprise Manager 10*g*
Client System Analyzer

This page will deploy the Oracle Client System Analyzer to your computer. The CSA applet will collect information about your computer's configuration, such as the hard drive size, CPU speed, memory, and installed software. It will also perform some network performance measurements. Your Java Virtual Machine will prompt you to accept the applet. Click "Yes" to accept it and run CSA.

Note that the applet may have been customized by the server administrator, and may perform additional tasks. In this case, the applet will not be signed by Oracle Corporation, but by the company using this product.

Gathering Client Configuration Data . . . . . Done

Performing Network Performance Measurements . . . . . Done

Posting Results Back to Server . . . . . Done

View Results

Figure 4-8. *Client System Analyzer*

Manually Analyzing the Client

If the Client System Analyzer is unavailable for your use, many of the steps can be performed manually.

Some of the key areas where client systems may encounter resource constraints are memory and CPU usage, and data on this usage can be obtained for the client using Windows Task Manager. Pressing the Ctrl, Alt, and Del keys simultaneously will initiate the Windows Task Manager. Select the Performance tab to display CPU Usage and Memory Usage charts, as shown in Figure 4-9.

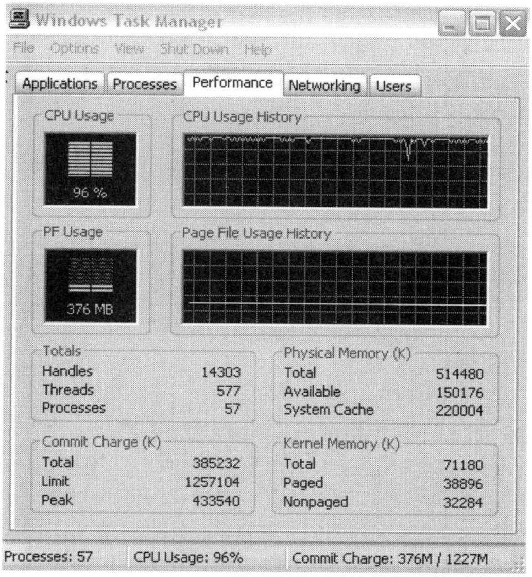

Figure 4-9. *The Performance tab of Windows Task Manager*

If either chart shows excessive usage, select the Processes tab to view running processes. This display can be sorted by the CPU or Mem Usage columns in order to identify resource-intensive processes. For example, this investigation could show a virus scanning utility consuming high amounts of CPU that results in client-level performance problems running Oracle Application Forms.

Trace Files

Generating and analyzing trace files is an important step of the performance tuning process. Analyzing trace files is the only way the Applications DBA and development staff can see what is being executed via the application in the database. Also, generating trace files is typically a requirement when providing feedback to Oracle Support.

Generating Trace Files

Trace files can be generated for any process that is executed in the application. Trace files are useful in generating explain plans for all queries that are executed, and explain plans can identify problem queries and assist Oracle Development in providing fixes to application code.

A raw trace file can be generated for either a Forms or Self Service application, as outlined in the following two sections. After tracing has been set up, reproduce the steps in the application where the performance degradation is being experienced. This will capture pertinent information in the trace file that will assist in determining the cause of the performance issues. Be certain to turn tracing off after the trace file has been generated.

■**Note** Generated trace files are located in the directory specified by the `user_dump_dest` database initialization parameter. For more information regarding this parameter, see Chapter 2 of this guide.

Forms Trace Files

To generate a trace file for a Form, be sure to have the profile options `Utilities: Diagnostics` set to `Yes` and `Hide Diagnostics Menu Entry` set to No. Log on to the application, and select the Help ➤ Diagnostic ➤ Trace ➤ Trace with Binds and Waits menu option. After this, you should set the trace size to unlimited by selecting the following menu option: Help ➤ Diagnostics ➤ Trace ➤ Unlimited Trace File Size. The resulting trace file will be written to the `udump` directory located on the Database Node.

Self Service Trace Files

Self Service Tracing can be implemented by navigating to Security ➤ Profile ➤ User. Enter the user name. Query the profile FND: Diagnostics. Set FND: Diagnostics to Yes. Log in to the application as the user for which the diagnostics profile was set. Click the diagnostics icon, select Set Trace Level, and click Go. On the next page, select Trace with Binds and Waits, and click Save.

Perform the steps required to duplicate the problem. When this has been completed, there will be a trace file generated. This file can be located and analyzed using the techniques explained in the next section.

Analyzing Trace Files

Once the raw trace file has been generated, execute the `tkprof` or `trcanlzr` utilities to translate it into a readable format. Descriptions for using these utilities are provided in the following sections.

Using tkprof

In order to run tkprof on the raw trace file, obtain the name of the generated trace file. Note that tkprof may only be executed in the database from which the trace file was originally generated. Execute tkprof as the instance owner in a directory with write permissions as follows:

```
$tkprof <raw trace file name> <output filename> \
explain=apps/<apps password>
```

The file generated by tkprof will contain important information regarding the SQL statement, as well as diagnostics that include CPU and elapsed time, disk and logical reads, and the number of rows returned in the query, as well as the SQL execution plan. Most likely, this file will need to be uploaded to Oracle Support for assistance in resolving the underlying performance issue.

The following is an example of output generated by executing tkprof:

```
SELECT USER_NAME
FROM FND_USER
WHERE USER_ID = :B1
```

call	count	cpu	elapsed	disk	query	current	rows
Parse	1	0.00	0.00	0	0	0	0
Execute	1	0.00	0.00	0	0	0	0
Fetch	1	0.00	0.00	0	3	0	1
total	3	0.00	0.00	0	3	0	1

```
Misses in library cache during parse: 1
Optimizer goal: CHOOSE
Parsing user id: 60     (recursive depth: 1)
```

Rows	Row Source Operation
1	TABLE ACCESS BY INDEX ROWID FND_USER

■Tip Setting the _user_files_public database initialization parameter will set trace file permissions such that users other than the instance owner can view the raw trace file and generate tkprof analysis of it.

Using trcanlzr

The Trace Analyzer utility (trcanlzr) reads a raw trace and generates an HTML report that includes tkprof analysis data as well as other statistics. The HTML file that is generated can be used by Oracle Support to assist in resolving performance issues.

To generate the HTML file, the trcanlzr utility must be downloaded from Oracle Support. It is available by referencing MetaLink Note 224270.1. Once the utility has been downloaded, you will need to install it by following the instructions in the download.

Analyzing SQL Statements in Oracle10*g*

Oracle Database 10*g* provides some additional tools for analyzing SQL statements beyond generating trace files. These tools may be used for tuning custom code as well as identifying issues with Oracle-provided code.

SQL Tuning Advisor

Along with the automatic database analysis tools introduced in Oracle10*g*, there is now an SQL Tuning Advisor (STA) whose purpose is to automate the SQL tuning process. The STA will analyze SQL statements for areas of improvement, looking for the same issues that the DBA would look for manually. Problems such as stale statistics, poor execution paths, and poorly structured SQL statements will be identified by the automatic analysis.

As with the other automatic analysis tools, Oracle recommends using Enterprise Manager as the primary interface with the tool. However, it is still possible to manually execute the tool using the DBMS_SQLTUNE package. To manually use the STA to tune an SQL statement, use the CREATE_TUNING_TASK function followed by the EXECUTE_TUNING_TASK function. When the tuning task has been executed, a report can be generated. Here is an example:

```
sql>exec dbms_sqltune.create_tuning_task( -
>sql_text => 'select * from emp where emp_id=101', -
>user_name => 'SCOTT', -
>scope => 'COMPREHENSIVE', -
>time_limit => 60, -
>task_name => 'tune_emp', -
>description => 'Task to tune a query on the EMP table')
```

```
sql>exec dbms_sqltune.execute_tuning_task (task_name => 'tune_emp')
```

```
sql>select dbms_sqltune.report_tuning_task('tune_emp') from dual;
```

The output of the tuning report may include recommendations such as analyzing the emp table if the statistics are invalid.

SQL Access Advisor

While STA is useful for tuning individual SQL statements, there is often a need to tune multiple queries. This tuning effort is possible through the use of the SQL Access Advisor (SAA). The SAA tool will analyze multiple statements and recommend the creation of objects such as indexes and materialized views to improve the overall performance of the queries. The group of queries to be tuned is called a SQL Tuning Set (STS).

Running SAA is a simple process if you use the Enterprise Manager. To run SAA manually, you will need to perform the following steps:

1. Create AWR snapshots before and after the group of queries is executed. Use the following command to generate each snapshot:

```
sql>exec dbms_workload_repository.create_snapshot()
```

2. After the beginning and ending snapshots are taken, create an STS using the following command:

```
sql>exec dbms_sqltune.create_sqlset('sts1')
```

3. Load the queries into the STS created in step 2. The following example limits the queries loaded into the STS to queries with relatively high disk reads:

```
sql>declare
  2   baseline_ref_cursor dbms_sqltune.sqlset_cursor;
  3   begin
  4      open baseline_ref_cursor for
  5         select value(p) from table
  6         (dbms_sqltune.select_workload_repository
  7         (:snap_id_1, :snap_id_2, 'disk_reads > 100',
  8         NULL, 'disk_reads')) p;
  9      dbms_sqltune.load_sqlset('sts1', baseline_ref_cursor);
 10   end;
 11/
```

4. Create an SQL workload to hold the STS:

```
sql>exec dbms_advisor.create_sqlwkld('sts_wkld1')
sql>variable saved_queries number;
sql>variable failed_queries number;
sql>begin
2 dbms_advisor.import_sqlwkld_sts( 'sts_wkld1', 'sts1'
3 ,'NEW', 1,:saved_queries, :failed_queries);
4 end;
5 /
```

5. Create a tuning task for the SAA:

```
sql>variable task_id number;
sql>begin
  2    dbms_advisor.create_task('SQL Access Advisor',
  3    :task_id, 'sql_task1');
  4 end;
  5/
```

6. Associate the SQL workload with the tuning task created in step 5, and execute the tuning task:

```
sql>exec dbms_advisor.add_sqlwkld_ref('sql_task1', 'sts_wkld1')
sql>exec dbms_advisor.execute_task('sql_task1')
```

7. Create a script of the recommendations from SAA. Before this can be done, a directory needs to be created to store the script. This should be done at the operating system level and then be added to DBA_DIRECTORIES.

```
sql>create directory saa_results as '/tmp/saa_results';
sql>exec dbms_advisor.create_file(dbms_advisor.get_task_script -
>( 'sql_task1' ), 'SAA_RESULTS', 'sts_script.sql')
```

The script created, /tmp/saa_results/sts_script.sql, can be executed in a test environment to implement the SAA recommendations. Before executing the script, however, the Applications DBA should review the recommendations. If the changes result in improvement, they can be promoted to production.

Additional Tuning Considerations

There are additional application profiles that may affect the performance of the application. Some of these profiles affect the behavior of the application, while others are diagnostic and logging settings. The profile options to review are outlined in Table 4-13.

Table 4-13. *Additional Profile Options to Consider for Performance Tuning*

Profile	Recommended Value	Description
ICX: Match case view	checked or hidden	This profile option controls queries that would disable indexes with the upper clause in an advanced search. The default value of unchecked allows for poor-performing queries due to unused indexes.
FND: Diagnostics	No	This profile option controls whether users are able to turn on global diagnostics.
FND: Debug Log Module	%	This profile may be used to set logging for a specific application. If FND: Debug Log Level is set to STATEMENT, you must set this profile to a specific module; otherwise logging will cause severe performance degradation.
FND: Debug Log Enabled	Yes	This profile can enable or disable debug logging. When set in conjunction with the FND: Debug Log Level profile, this profile controls whether information is logged.
FND: Debug Log Level	UNEXPECTED	This profile will write errors that occur in the application to the log file. When set to UNEXPECTED, only errors that require administrator assistance to resolve will be logged. Other values for this profile include STATEMENT, PROCEDURE, EVENT, EXCEPTION, and ERROR. When set in conjunction with the FND: Debug Log Enabled profile, this profile controls the amount of information that is logged.

Common Performance Issues

Performance issues are often a result of preventative maintenance tasks not being performed. Key preventative maintenance tasks include generating statistics and recompiling invalid objects. Make certain that all required preventative maintenance is properly executed. When in doubt, refresh the database statistics. Chapter 6 of this guide contains additional information on recommended preventative maintenance.

Frequently, performance issues are experienced when the user community is using new functionality. It is imperative that new features be performance tested before being turned on in production. Along with testing new functionality, a stress test of the environment is necessary to ensure that available resources are adequate. The Applications DBA should work with the user community and development team to create a realistic stress test using stress-test software.

It is impossible to gauge the impact of additional users and new functionality on the production environment without a properly developed stress-test plan. When monitoring the stress test, use Statspack or AWR to identify potential problems. Also use database monitoring tools and operating system monitoring tools to determine whether memory and CPU resources are adequate. Additional hardware may be needed to support the required functionality.

Performance Tuning Best Practices

For overall application health, it is important to stay current with patches and upgrades for the technology stack components. Often patches and later versions of the technology stack include performance improvements, as well as additional configuration options. The Applications DBA should monitor and apply current releases for AD, FND, and the ATG Product Family. Oracle provides MetaLink Note 244040.1, titled "Oracle E-Business Suite Recommended Performance Patches," and this note should be regularly reviewed for recommended patches.

The Applications DBA should work with the user community to identify commonly used modules. Document typical execution timings for the functionality of all commonly used modules. These timings should be reviewed and updated when patches specific to that module are applied to the application. This level of documentation will provide a baseline of performance expectations for the application.

As previously stated, stress testing is critical for the success of any application. Stress tests provide an environment that will simulate production and determine whether additional resources are necessary in order to meet business requirements. Stress tests should be implemented when upgrading, applying patches that change the underlying technology stack components, and implementing new functionality.

While resolving performance issues, it is often necessary to work with Oracle Support and Development. When doing so, provide all applicable reports (Statspack, AWR, and/or trace files) in addition to other statistics that have been collected. Also provide a detailed description of the performance degradation that is being experienced, including screen shots of the process if applicable. All of this information will assist Oracle in resolving the issue. Although rare, it may be necessary for Oracle to release a one-off perform-ance patch for the issue being experienced. It is advisable to log an SR when the performance issue is first experienced in order to expedite resolution from Oracle if an underlying code change is required.

CHAPTER 5

■■■

Patching

One of the most important and time-consuming aspects of an Oracle Applications DBA's job is applying patches to the E-Business Suite. Patches may be required to resolve problems with the application code, to fix production issues, to install new features, or to upgrade components of the technology stack. Patching is not a simple one-step process, but rather requires careful research in order to determine all of the prerequisite steps, patching steps, and post-patching steps required.

Oracle E-Business Suite patching can be divided into two categories:

- **Oracle Applications patching**: This includes all patching that changes the underlying Oracle Applications code.

- **Technology stack components patching**: This includes all upgrades and fixes for the Oracle Database software, JDK, Oracle Developer 6*i* (Oracle Forms and Reports), Developer 6*i* Client library files, Oracle Discoverer, JDBC, Oracle Java Server Page (OJSP), Oracle Application Server (iAS), and iAS Client library files (Required Support Files or RSF).

The focus of this chapter will be on Oracle Applications patching, and a brief overview of Oracle Database software patching will also be provided. Patching the Applications Technology Stack will not be covered, as this type of patching effort has numerous operating system dependencies.

Applications Patching

There are several steps involved in patching Oracle Applications. In this section we'll discuss each of these stages:

- **Preparing to patch**: Before patching, it is important to document the requirements and determine what steps and patches are needed. This section will explain how to document and manage the overall process of applying patches, and discuss patch reporting, where you investigate which version, if any, of a patch is currently installed.

- **Applying patches**: Applying a patch involves several steps, such as unbundling the patch, enabling maintenance mode, applying the patch with adpatch, and implementing manual steps. This section will discuss each of the steps involved.

- **Monitoring and resolving patching issues**: Sometimes there are problems applying patches. This section will explain how to review log files and use the AD Control utility to monitor patch worker processes.

- **Post-patching steps and cleaning up**: There are often steps that should be performed after the patching is complete. This section will explain how you can efficiently perform post-patching steps and clean up files no longer required after patching.

Types of Application Patches

There are several different types of Oracle Applications patches. These are the more common patches:

- **One-off patch**: This is the simplest type of patch. It is created to resolve a specific bug.

- **Minipack patch**: This is a collection of one-off patches and enhancements related to a particular module. Alphabetic characters denote the Minipack version for the module; for example, the product code for the Application DBA utilities is AD, and version Minipack I of this product would be called AD.I.

- **Family Pack patch**: This is a collection of Minipack patches for a particular family group of application modules. Alphabetic characters denote the Family Pack version; for example, the J version of the Human Resources Suite Product Family would be HR_PF.J.

- **Maintenance Pack patch**: This is a collection of Family Packs that serves as a point-level release upgrade; Oracle Applications Release 11.5.10 is an example of a Maintenance Pack.

There are also other special types of patches:

- **Consolidated patch**: This is a collection of one-off fixes for a Family Pack or Maintenance Pack; Oracle Applications 11.5.10 Consolidated Update 2 (CU2) is an example of a consolidated patch.

- **Interoperability patch**: This is a patch that is required for Oracle Applications to function with a newer version of a technology stack component; for example, you would apply an interoperability patch when upgrading the database to version 10*g*.

- **NLS patch**: This is a patch that updates language-specific information for multi-language installations.

- **Rollup patch**: This is a collection of one-off patches that update code levels for particular products.

- **Legislative patch**: This is a special patch for HR Payroll customers; it contains legislative data for multiple countries.

As the patch group size increases from one-off patches to Maintenance Packs, the complexity of the patch application process also increases. More research is required for Family Packs than is required for a Minipack. Due to the increased complexity, there is more planning required for Maintenance Packs and Family Packs than other patches.

Preparing to Patch

Before applying a patch, carefully examine the readme file provided with the patch. This document will list all steps required by the patch.

■**Tip** Before applying a patch, make certain that the readme file has been carefully reviewed.

The readme file will contain prerequisites, installation steps, postinstallation steps, and other information vital to the successful installation of the patch. The prerequisites may consist of other patches or manual steps. Here is an example of the readme file contents:

```
----------------------------------------------------------------
README CONTENTS:
----------------------------------------------------------------
```

```
A. Prerequisites
B. Best Practices
C. Installation Steps
D. Post-Installation Steps
E. HRGLOBAL - SPECIAL NOTES AND CHANGE HISTORY
F. Other Information Sources
----------------------------------------------------------------------
A. PREREQUISITES:
----------------------------------------------------------------------
Apply this patch if you have HR (Product code PER) fully installed.

Before applying this patch you must have each of these prerequisites:

1. Oracle Applications Server 11i

2. Oracle 11i.PER.G, patch 1988754, or later.
. . .
```

If prerequisites have not been met, you must add these steps or patches to the overall process of applying the patch. Become familiar with all steps required before attempting to apply the patch.

■Caution Removing a patch from Oracle Applications after it has been applied is not usually a feasible option; therefore, a full system backup should be taken before applying patches to an instance.

Documenting the Patching Process

It is recommended that you maintain a spreadsheet detailing all prerequisite steps, patching steps, and post-installation steps required for patch application. By creating such a document, you can eliminate operator error, such as missed steps or steps completed out of order.

The columns in the spreadsheet should be customized to match your needs. These columns can include information about the node being patched, details about the patch being applied, or the rationale for the patch. At a minimum, it is useful to have columns for patch number, description, and comments, but it is often also useful to include the actual time required to complete each step based upon trial runs in a sandbox instance. Tracking timings allows for an accurate prediction of production maintenance downtime.

Figure 5-1 shows an example of a spreadsheet for patches required by Project A that will require 6 hours and 25 minutes to apply.

	A	B	C	D	E
1	Patches Required for Project A				
2	Patch#	Description	Comment	Time Required	Shift Start time
3					
4		Stop Application processes		0:15	10/13/06 7:00 PM
5		Put application in Maintenance mode	use ADADMIN	0:05	10/13/06 7:15 PM
6	111111	Patch 1	prerequisite for patch 111112	1:30	10/13/06 7:20 PM
7	111112	Patch 2		0:45	10/13/06 8:50 PM
8		run /patch/script/project_a/post_111112.sh	post step for patch 1111112	0:30	10/13/06 9:35 PM
9	111113	Patch 3	resolves issue from TAR 1223334.987	2:00	10/13/06 10:05 PM
10		Take application out of Maintenance mode	use ADADMIN	0:05	10/14/06 12:05 AM
11		Recompile Invalid objects	use ADADMIN	0:30	10/14/06 12:10 AM
12		Restart Application processes		0:15	10/14/06 12:40 AM
13		Validate Application before contacting testers.		0:30	10/14/06 12:55 AM
14			Time to complete->	6:25	10/14/06 1:25 AM

Figure 5-1. *Sample patch documentation spreadsheet*

If timings are included for every step, the Applications DBA can generate a schedule for applying the patches to production by using time functions in the spreadsheet software. This corresponds to the Shift Start Time column in Figure 5-1. This process is highly recommended for extended patching efforts that will require multiple shifts. Otherwise, a simple summation of the time required for each step should provide an accurate schedule. The times required for applying patches is also tracked by adpatch and can be found in the `$APPL_TOP/admin/$CONTEXT_NAME.out/adt*.lst` files.

■**Tip** When documenting the patching process for multiple patches, post-installation steps like recompiling invalid objects, regenerating JAR files, and running the autoconfig utility can be consolidated and executed at the end of the patching process. This helps to streamline the patch process and reduce downtime.

Patch Reporting

Patch reporting is used to determine whether or not a specific patch has already been applied to the instance, or what version of a Family Pack or Minipack is currently installed. The following sections will discuss four methods for determining patching levels:

- Using the adphrept.sql script
- Executing the patchsets.sh utility
- Querying the database
- Using Oracle Application Manager (OAM)

Using adphrept.sql

The $AD_TOP/patch/115/sql/adphrept.sql file is an Oracle-provided script for generating a patch report for an instance. This script provides an easily searchable list of all patches that have been applied to an environment. Keep in mind that the script can take a long time to execute.

Additional details regarding adphrept.sql and a description of all parameters can be obtained by viewing MetaLink Note 162498.1. The parameters for adphrept.sql are shown in Table 5-1.

Table 5-1. adphrept.sql *Parameters*

Option	Purpose
Query_depth	1—Lists details of patches only
	2—Lists details of patches and their bug fixes only
	3—Lists details of patches, their bug fixes, and bug actions
Bug_number	Lists details for one bug number or ALL
Bug_product	Lists details for one product or ALL
End_date_from	Lists start date for a date range or ALL
End_date_to	Lists end date for a date range or ALL
Patchname	Lists details for a patch name or ALL
Patchtype	Lists details for a patch type or ALL
Level	Lists details for a patch level or ALL
Language	Lists details for a language or ALL
Appltop	Lists details for a specific APPL_TOP or ALL
Limit to forms server	Limits the list's scope (Y/N)
Limit to web server	Limits the list's scope (Y/N)

Option	Purpose
Limit to node server	Limits the list's scope (Y/N)
Limit to admin server	Limits the list's scope (Y/N)
Only patches that change db	Limits the list's scope (Y/N)
Report name	Specifies the report name; it must end in .txt or .htm

Typically, the report is executed with Query_depth set to 2 and all other options set either as ALL or Y. This will yield the most useful report for prerequisite requirement searching. The query must be run by the apps user account, like this:

```
$sqlplus apps/apps_password \
@adphrept.sql 2 ALL ALL ALL ALL ALL \
ALL ALL ALL ALL N N N N N patches.txt
```

■**Tip** As of Application Utility Minipack version I (AD.I), adphrept.sql no longer generates a text report, but rather an XML report is generated.

To search the report for a specific patch or bug, the following may be executed against the generated file:

```
grep [patch or bug number] patches.txt
```

If the grep command returns results, the patch or bug fix has been applied to the instance. For example, to test for existence of patch 3410000, check whether the following command returns any data:

```
$grep 3410000 patches.txt
```

Using patchsets.sh

The Oracle-provided patch-comparison utility, patchsets.sh, is a handy tool for reviewing patchset levels. Family Pack versions, fully installed products, and shared installed products, along with the latest version available, are displayed in the output. Information about the latest version of this utility can be reviewed in MetaLink Note 139684.1.

This utility is updated frequently by Oracle. Before running the script, download the current version from the following FTP site: ftp://oracle-ftp. oracle.com/apps/patchsets/PATCHSET_COMPARE_TOOL/patchsets.sh.

The instance owner can use the tool by executing the following:

```
patchsets.sh connect=[userid]/[password]
```

Here's an example:

```
$patchsets.sh connect=apps/apps_password
```

More details about the parameters available for this script can be found by using the -h parameter for online help. Figure 5-2 shows an example of the output of patchsets.sh from MetaLink Note 139684.1.

The output for the file will contain the following columns for each product group:

- **Baseline Version**: Displays the version provided with the release.
- **Running Version**: Displays the current version installed for each product.
- **Latest Available, Status**: Displays the current version available for the product. The Status portion of the column consists of two parts: the patchset status (Rel is short for released, Sup for superseded, and Obs for obsoleted) and the distribution status (By_Metal indicates it is on MetaLink, Not_Dist means it is not available, and By_Dev means it is available from development only).

Review the output to find any products that have updates available.

Querying the Database for Patches

In order to determine whether a specific patch has been applied, a query can be executed against the bug_number table. The following SQL will return results if the patches included in the IN clause have been applied to the instance:

```
SELECT bug_number
FROM ad_bugs
WHERE bug_number IN ('patch_number', 'patch_number', . . .)
ORDER BY bug_number DESC;
```

Using OAM

Oracle Application Manager (OAM) may also be used to query the instance for applied patches.

```
==============================================================================
        Report Generated: Tue Apr 19 12:17:10 EDT 2005          Tool Version:  4.19
    Patchsets List Updated: Apr 18 22:30
...
            Program Updates: ftp://oracle-ftp/apps/patchsets/PATCHSET_COMPARE_TOOL/
        Download Patchsets: Go to link below or click on Patches
        http://metalink.oracle.com/metalink/plsql/dis_download.startup
==============================================================================

                                FAMILY PACK PATCHES
Product Baseline Version        Running Version         Latest Available,Status
------- ----------------        ---------------         ------------------------
atg_pf                                                  11i.ATG_PF.H(3438354), Rel-By_Metal
bis_pf                                                  11i.BIS_PF.D.1(4054609), Rel-By_Metal
...
dmf_pf  11i.DMF_PF.E(1745355)   11i.DMF_PF.E(1745355)   11i.DMF_PF.J(2771139), Rel-Not_Dist
exchg_pf                                                11i.EXCHG_PF.C(2147366), Rel-By_Metal
fin_pf                          11i.FIN_PF.C(2380068)   11i.FIN_PF.F(3153675), Rel-By_Metal
...

                                FULLY INSTALLED PRODUCTS
Product Baseline Version        Running Version         Latest Available,Status
------- ----------------        ---------------         ------------------------
ak      11i.AK.C(1553747)       11i.AK.C(1553747)       11i.AK.G(3263645), Rel-By_Metal
alr     11i.ALR.C(1575525)      11i.ALR.C(1575525)      11i.ALR.G(3261254), Rel-By_Metal
ams     11i.AMS.B(1339203)      11i.AMS.C(1568669)      11i.AMS.I(3025816), Rel-Not_Dist
...

                                SHARED INSTALL PRODUCTS
Product Baseline Version        Running Version         Latest Available,Status
------- ----------------        ---------------         ------------------------
ad      11i.AD.D(1627493)       11i.AD.D(1627493)       11i.AD.I.1(4038964), Rel-By_Metal
amv     11i.AMV.D(1615230)      11i.AMV.D(1615230)      11i.AMV.I(3134012), Rel-Not_Dist
asg     11i.ASG.D(1580949)      11i.ASG.D(1580949)      11i.ASG.R(3263401), Rel-By_Metal
...

                                PSEUDO PRODUCTS
Product Baseline Version        Running Version         Latest Available,Status
------- ----------------        ---------------         ------------------------
adx                                                     11i.ADX.E.1(3817226), Rel-By_Metal
...
oie     11i.OIE.B(1633913)      11i.OIE.E(1960506)      11i.OIE.J(3618125), Rel-By_Metal
oir                             11i.OIR.C(2396507)      11i.OIR.F(3151380), Rel-By_Metal
oit     11i.OIT.B(1675976)      11i.OIT.B(1675976)      11i.OIT.D(2397276), Rel-By_Metal
owf                                                     11i.OWF.H(3258819), Rel-By_Metal
,...
```

Figure 5-2. *Output from the* patchsets.sh *script*

Patch Search In OAM, the Applied Patches functionality will allow searches by Patch ID, Applied From Date, and Applied to Date. Once a search result is returned, additional details regarding the patch can be displayed.

For example, the Simple Search screen for patches in OAM is shown in Figure 5-3.

Figure 5-3. *The OAM Simple Search screen*

The Advanced Search screen offers additional search criteria. Use this screen if you need to search for certain product families, patches applied only to certain nodes, or patches for different APPL_TOPs.

When a patch is returned to the result screen, you can select the Details cell to see a patch-impact analysis screen. This information can be useful to testers for determining functionality that was altered by the patch. For large patches, the patch-impact analysis may be too lengthy to be of much value.

Patch Advisor OAM can also be used to perform patch analysis reporting against your instance. Select the Patch Wizard Tasks menu to see the options shown in Figure 5-4.

Patch Wizard : **VIS**

Last Updated : 02-10-2005 15:45:30 🗈

Patch Wizard Tasks

Task Name	Description	Tasks	Job Status
Patch Wizard Preferences	Set download, merge, and stage area preferences	⬛	
Define Patch Filters	Create custom patch filters	⬛	
Recommend/Analyze Patches	Submit requests for patch advice or analysis	⬛	▥
Download Patches	Submit requests to download patches	⬛	▥

Figure 5-4. *The Patch Wizard Tasks menu*

Select Patch Wizard Preferences to define your work environment. These options include the staging directory for patches, as well as language and platform defaults. The Patch Wizard will use these details to download information from MetaLink in order to create recommendations or patch analysis.

A scheduled job can be created to perform these tasks on a regular basis, as shown in Figure 5-5.

Schedule
ⓘ If no date or an earlier date is specified, the request will be scheduled to run immediately.

Date [02-10-2005] 🗓
      (dd-MM-yyyy)

Time [00 ▾] [00 ▾]

Recurrence
◉ Never Repeat

◯ Repeat
  Every [   ] [Days ▾]
End Date [   ] 🗓
          (dd-MM-yyyy)
End Time [00 ▾] [00 ▾]

Figure 5-5. *Scheduling options for patch analysis*

Applying Patches

After all of the required patching steps have been documented, you can begin the process of applying the patch. This generally involves the following logical steps:

1. Download and unbundle the patch.
2. Identify patch drivers required for the patch.
3. Place the instance in maintenance mode.
4. Use the AD Patch utility to apply patch driver files.
5. Perform any manual steps that may be required.

A sandbox instance is a must for applying patches. This instance gives the Oracle Applications DBA a place to apply patches and resolve issues without impacting production or other test instances. Ensure that the sandbox is a recent clone of production, so that this environment matches the production environment. All steps should be practiced multiple times and be thoroughly tested before applying the patch in production.

■**Note** The adpatch utility must be run as the owner of the application software.

Unbundling the Patch

The first step is to download the patch and unbundle it using an unzip utility. If errors are encountered while unzipping large zip files, you may require an updated version of the unzip program. Review operating system specifics and release notes regarding the unzip utility.

It is advisable to have a separate filesystem for storing and unbundling patches. When a large patch, such as a maintenance pack, is released, a temporary filesystem may need to be created to store the unbundled patch. When sizing the filesystem, be sure to include an extra 20 percent for backup information that is written to the patch directory.

■**Tip** Before applying a patch, confirm that there is enough space allocated to the instance filesystem, as well as to the filesystem where the patch has been unbundled. Exhausting filesystem space is a common error that occurs while applying patches.

Identifying Patch Drivers

Patches consist of a combination of a c, d, and/or g driver, or a unified u driver, that is applied to all appropriate nodes using the adpatch utility.

The c driver is the copy driver. This driver is used to update the filesystem with new file versions. The d driver is the database driver. It is used to update database level code and objects. The g driver is the generate driver. It is used to generate forms, PL/SQL libraries, reports, and menus. It is imperative that if a patch contains c, d, or g drivers, that they are applied in alphabetical order: c, d, g.

The u driver is a merged driver that is a combined c, d, and/or g driver. Oracle is beginning to release a majority of its patches as unified driver patches. If a patch is a unified driver patch, then only the u driver is applied. The naming convention for patch driver files is u[Patch#].drv.

Once the patch has been downloaded and unbundled, change directory to the location where the patch driver(s) is located in preparation for applying the patch using the adpatch utility. Before you do, though, you should switch the instance to maintenance mode.

Enabling Maintenance Mode

Most patches require the application processes be shut down prior to applying the patch. As of release AD.I the system is required to be in Maintenance Mode prior to applying patches.

The instance can be placed in maintenance mode by running adadmin and selecting the appropriate menu options. Executing the SQL script $AD_TOP/patch/115/sql/adsetmmd.sql with the ENABLE parameter will place the instance in maintenance mode without using adadmin. When the patching has been completed, be sure to take the instance out of Maintenance Mode by executing $AD_TOP/patch/115/sql/adsetmmd.sql with the DISABLE parameter, or by using the adadmin utility.

A patch can also be applied using the hotpatch parameter. This option does not require the instance to be in Maintenance Mode, however Oracle recommends using Maintenance Mode to improve patching performance.

Using AD Patch

The administrative tool used to apply application patches is AD Patch, also referred to by its command line executable, adpatch. Basic information about the AD Patch utility can be found in Oracle MetaLink Note 181665.1, "REL11i ADPATCH BASICS." The AD Patch utility will spawn off a user-determined number of worker threads or patch worker processes to update application code by copying later versions of programs to the application tier; updating database objects, regeneration application forms, and reports; and performing some post-patching steps. The code changes are determined by the patch's driver files.

■**Tip** Prior to executing `adpatch`, disable any password constraints defined within the application or database. These constraints could cause errors if the patch creates a new user account. You may also need to reset some standard Oracle passwords for accounts such as `CTXSYS`.

An Oracle Applications DBA needs to be familiar with the options available for the AD Patch utility. The parameters supported by the `adpatch` command differ depending upon the AD Minipack level applied with Oracle Applications. When upgrading the AD product group, be sure to identify and understand any new features of the AD Patch utility. Study the `adpatch` command parameters for any possible benefits. Use the command `adpatch help=y` to see the available options.

In order to enable an option with `adpatch`, use the following syntax:

```
adpatch options=[option1, option2..]
```

The `adpatch` options shown in Table 5-2 are commonly used to accelerate the patching process.

Table 5-2. *Commonly Used* adpatch *Options*

Option	Purpose
Novalidate	Prevents adpatch from validating all schema connections
Noprereq	Prevents adpatch from checking the existence of prerequisite patches
Nocompiledb	Prevents adpatch from compiling database objects
Nocompilejsp	Prevents adpatch from compiling JSP objects
Noautoconfig	Prevents adpatch from running autoconfig after the patch has completed
Nogenerateportion	Prevents adpatch from compiling forms, menus, and plls
Hidepw	Prevents passwords from being displayed in log files
Hotpatch	Allows adpatch to be run when the instance is not in maintenance mode

▉**Tip** If you are applying a large number of patches, use the options `nocompilejsp`, `nocompiledb`, `noprereq`, and `novalidate` to speed up the application of the patches. Recompiling Java Server Pages (JSP) pages and database objects can be performed at the end of the patching process. In this situation, placing the database in `noarchivelog` mode may also improve patching performance.

Having changed directory to the location where the patch driver(s) is located, you can then start the patching session as the instance owner by executing `adpatch` with the desired options:

```
adpatch options=nocompiledb,novalidate
```

When `adpatch` is started, the user must respond to several questions. These questions serve to verify application file settings, database connectivity, and patch driver options. For example, the user may set `adpatch` to send an email upon failure. The following questions from `adpatch` require additional explanation:

Question: Filename for AutoPatch Log

Recommended response: Rather than use the default name of `adpatch.log`, use a more descriptive name, such as `[c|d|g|u][patch#].log`. For multi-node or multi-language patching, you should consider including the server name and language in the filename. Additional descriptions may also be added depending on your environment.

Question: The default directory is [current working directory]

Recommended response: It is advised that you run the `adpatch` utility from the directory where the patch has been unbundled. By doing this, the default value for this question can be chosen. Otherwise, enter the directory where the patch was unbundled.

Question: Please enter the name of your AutoPatch driver file

Recommended response: This depends upon the patch being applied. Most patches from Oracle now contain a single u driver. If the patch contains c, d, and/or g drivers, `adpatch` needs to be run for each driver. The drivers need to be applied in alphabetical order.

Question: Number of parallel workers

Recommended response: This value is environment-specific and should be adjusted accordingly.

Using a defaultsfile will allow for noninteractive patching by providing responses to the adpatch questions. The defaultsfile option of adpatch must point to a file in the $APPL_TOP/admin/$CONTEXT_NAME directory. This option is typically used with the mode interactive=no.

Performing Manual Steps

If any part of the patching process requires numerous manual steps, it is useful to create scripts to automate the manual commands. This can not only help reduce the chances of human error during the patching process, but scripting can also speed up the process.

For ease of management, you should create a special directory to be the home directory for such scripts. During the creation of the scripts, be sure to include logging commands as well as parameters for values such as instance name. When you parameterize such variables, the scripts can be executed with each patching effort without requiring modifications.

For example, you may build a script of manual steps that looks similar to the following template:

```
SCRIPT_TOP=/patch/scripts/project_a
INSTANCE_NAME=$1
LOG_TOP=$SCRIPT_TOP/logs
script_1.sh > $LOG_TOP/post_steps.log
command_1 >>$LOG_TOP/post_steps.log
script_2.sh $INSTANCE_NAME >> $LOG_TOP/post_steps.log
exit
```

In the preceding example, script_1.sh may be a script that performs a backup of library files, and script_2.sh could be a script that relinks several forms.

When the script has executed, thoroughly review the log files generated by the script. New failures may be encountered on some instances that had not occurred during past patch applications. Resolve any errors before proceeding to the next steps. Scripts created for such steps should contain error handling, such as checking the number and types of parameters Custom scripts should also contain documentation to describe the purpose of the script.

The scripts you create should be included in the spreadsheet as part of the process for applying the patch. Part of the documentation process for the patching effort involves using descriptive script and variable names.

Writing scripts is a useful skill set for Applications DBAs. We recommend you practice coding scripts on test servers while connected as a user with a low level of permissions until you become more comfortable with scripting. Always test your scripts thoroughly before running them on production systems.

Special Considerations

There are some additional issues that may need to be addressed during the patching process. A class of patches that contain legislative data has an additional driver called hrglobal, which may need to be applied. Also, for some groups of patches, it may be beneficial to merge the patches into one set of driver files. Depending upon your implementation, you may also need to deal with multi-language patches and multi-node patching. These topics are discussed in the following sections.

Applying Legislative Patches

For Oracle Payroll customers, there is another category of patch required by the system. The hrglobal patch supports the legislative requirements of multiple countries. Given the nature of this patch, it is updated frequently by Oracle. It is often a post-patch requirement for the mandatory patches released for Oracle Payroll.

To find the latest copy of the hrglobal patch, view MetaLink Note 145837.1. This note will contain the latest patch number for the hrglobal patch, along with a link to the patch installation instructions and a change history for the patch. The hrglobal patch can be downloaded from MetaLink like any other patch. Review the patch's readme file for required prerequisites.

After unpacking the patch, the adpatch utility can be run to install the patch's u driver. In addition to the u driver, these patches contain a special hrglobal driver. As a result of these differences, there are additional considerations for applying this type of patch.

Once the u driver has been applied, the DataInstall Java utility needs to be run in order to select needed legislations for install. The syntax for this command is as follows:

```
jre oracle.apps.per.DataInstall apps apps_password thin
[hostname]:[dbport]:[oracle_sid]
```

When the DataInstall utility has been executed, the Applications DBA will need to select all relevant legislations. Figure 5-6 shows the main menu for DataInstall.

```
+----------------------------------------------------+
|          DataInstall Main Menu                     |
+----------------------------------------------------+

1.    Select legislative data to install/upgrade

2.    Select college data to install/upgrade

3.    Select JIT/Geocode or OTL to install/upgrade

4.    Exit to confirmation menu
```

Figure 5-6. *The DataInstall Main Menu*

Select option 1 to choose which legislative data to install or upgrade. From the resulting menu, shown in Figure 5-7, you should choose to install any legislative data marked as installed. Note that the selection numbers will change depending upon your version of the hrglobal patch. Check the numbers for the appropriate data.

```
# Localisation        Product(s)                 Leg. Data? Action
- -------------------  -------------------------  ---------- -----------
1 Global               Human Resources            Installed
2 Australia            Human Resources
3 Australia            Payroll
...
55 United States       Human Resources            Installed
56 United States       Payroll                    Installed

   <Product #><Action> - Change Action
   where <Action> is [I : Install, C : Clear]
```

Figure 5-7. *The DataInstall legislative data submenu*

Select the legislative data to be installed by entering the localization number and I. If an incorrect number is selected, you can correct the mistake by entering that number with a C to clear the action.

After all legislative data is marked for install, return to the main menu to select any required college data. When all college data is selected, return to the main menu and select 4 to exit the utility. Upon exiting, an Actions Summary will be displayed. Review that summary to ensure that all required actions have been selected.

The final stage of the legislative patch is to run the adpatch utility to apply the hrglobal driver. This driver is copied to the $PER_TOP/patch/115/ driver directory by the patch's u driver. The same adpatch options for applying other drivers should be used for the hrglobal driver.

Using AD Merge

When applying a group of large patches, such as a Maintenance Pack and a cumulative update, some performance benefits can be incurred by using the AD Merge utility to combine the patches into one patch.

The set of patches to be merged should be copied to a common directory. After the patches are unbundled, the AD Merge utility can be run against the patches. Here is an example:

```
admrgpch /source_dir /target_dir
```

The completed merged driver files found in the target directory can be applied as a standard patch would be applied. The merged driver files will have a name like u_merged.drv. A log file, admrgpch.log, will be created in the directory where the utility was run.

For more information, see MetaLink Note 228779.1, "How to Merge Patches Using admrgpch." The admrgpch utility can be run with several parameters, shown in Table 5-3.

Table 5-3. admrgpch *Options*

Option	Purpose
s	Specifies the source directory containing compressed patch files.
d	Specifies the destination directory for merged patch files.
verbose	Controls the level of detail included in admrgpch output.
manifest	Specifies a text file containing the list of patch files to be merged. This is useful if the source directory includes a large number of patch files.
logfile	Specifies the log file to contain the output from admrgpch utility.
merge_name	Specifies the name of the merged file. This defaults to "merged", and it should be changed to be more descriptive.

When using this utility, thoroughly test the resulting patch.

Applying NLS Patches

For E-Business Suite installations with multiple language requirements, there are patches available for each additional language. Each required NLS patch needs to be applied to Oracle Applications. Oracle provides some recommendations for dealing with NLS patches; these are outlined in MetaLink Note 174436.1.

The U.S. version of the patch should be applied before any of the translation patches. The translation patches may be applied without downtime to the entire system if users of the affected language are not active.

Using admrgpch, it is possible to merge all U.S. patches into one patch, and then merge all non-U.S. patches into a separate patch. Depending upon the application configuration, some variation of this approach may be necessary.

Performing Multi-Node Patching

There are a couple of options available to optimize patching for multi-node environments. As of Oracle Applications 11.5.10, the system can be designed with a shared application-tier filesystem. The shared application filesystem contains the application's APPL_TOP, COMMON_TOP, and ORACLE_HOME. (MetaLink Note 233428.1 describes sharing the application-tier filesystem.) As a result of this configuration, patching the shared filesystem applies the patch to all nodes.

Prior to 11.5.10, a shared `APPL_TOP` did not include the `ORACLE_HOME`. For these systems, Forms and iAS patches must be applied to each Form and Web Node.

In order to increase the performance of the patching process, Distributed AD will execute workers on remote nodes in a multi-node implementation. Distributed AD improves scalability and resource utilization. Distributed AD is only available with AD Minipack H or later, and with a shared Application Tier Filesystem or shared `APPL_TOP`. More information on this feature can be found in MetaLink Note 236469.1.

If a shared Application Tier Filesystem is not in use, each filesystem will need to be patched separately. A patched filesystem can be cloned to another node if the downtime required to patch the node exceeds the time required to clone the filesystem.

Patch drivers have different requirements when applying them in a multi-node environment. The c driver must be applied to all `APPL_TOP`s, the d driver is applied on the Admin Node, the g driver is applied to all `APPL_TOP`s unless the `APPL_TOP` is only the Admin Node, and the u driver is applied to all `APPL_TOP`s on all nodes.

Monitoring and Resolving Patching Problems

Patching problems manifest themselves in many different ways. Typically the `adpatch` session will display an error or will appear to be hung on one task for a long period of time. The first step in resolving the issue is to review the `adpatch` log file and associated worker log file. Next, the reason the worker failed must be determined and resolved. After resolution has been obtained, `adctrl` can be used to continue the patching process.

Reviewing Log Files

During and after the application of patches, it is helpful to review log files of the `adpatch` session and its workers. These files are found in the `$APPL_TOP/admin/$CONTEXT_NAME/log` directory. The `adpatch` log filename is specified during the patch process. See the "Using AD Patch" section earlier in the chapter for more details.

In order to monitor the patch from a telnet session other than the one where the patch was started, a simple UNIX command such as `tail -f u[patch#].log` will display information as it is written to the log file. This is a useful means for monitoring the progress of a patch that is being applied.

The log files for the workers will be named `adwork[xxx].log`, where [xxx] is the number of the patch worker process. If a particular worker has failed, examine the related log file for detailed information. This information can be researched on MetaLink or used to open an SR with Oracle Support.

For example, the log file listing for the u driver of patch 11112, applied through adpatch using 5 workers, may look like this:

$ls

```
adwork001.log
adwork002.log
adwork003.log
adwork004.log
adwork005.log
u111112.log
```

Using AD Control

The administrative tool used to manage patch workers is AD Control, or adctrl. Frequently workers will fail or hang, which will require the Oracle Applications DBA to interface with adctrl. (Common patching errors will be covered later in this chapter.)

AD Control menu options will vary depending upon the AD patch version applied to the instance. When logged in as the application owner on the Admin Node, execute adctrl to display the menu options shown in Figure 5-8.

```
                    AD Controller Menu
-------------------------------------------------------------
1.      Show worker status
2.      Tell worker to restart a failed job
3.      Tell worker to quit
4.      Tell manager that a worker failed its job
5.      Tell manager that a worker acknowledges quit
6.      Restart a worker on the current machine
7.      Exit
```

Figure 5-8. *AD Controller Menu*

To execute an adctrl menu option, simply type the menu option and press Enter. If options 2–6 are chosen, either specify the number of the worker that requires action, or press Enter for the action to be executed for all workers.

The "Skip Worker" menu option is a hidden adctrl menu option. If a worker needs to be skipped, start adctrl, enter 8, and then enter the worker number. Only use this option if advised by Oracle Support.

■**Tip** With AD.I, `adctrl` may be used in noninteractive mode. Using `adctrl` noninteractively can expedite patch problem resolution.

Resolving AD Patch Worker Failure

If a worker has failed, the `adpatch` session will normally display a failed-worker message. The status of the worker may also be determined using `adctrl`. If a worker has failed, the worker error can be obtained by viewing the worker log file. Once the worker issue has been resolved, use `adctrl` to restart the worker.

If a worker has failed, and it is determined that the step the worker was trying to execute may be skipped, the hidden option 8 of the `adctrl` menu, "Skip Worker," may be used to skip the worker. It is only advisable to do this if the step is not critical to the environment being patched.

■**Tip** It may be necessary to research MetaLink or open an SR to resolve issues with failed workers. For additional information on MetaLink and the SR process, see Chapter 7 of this guide.

The following are common worker failures that will be seen by the Applications DBA during patching. The error messages will be displayed by the `adpatch` session or in the worker log file:

Error message: ORA-01013: user requested cancel of current operation

Resolution to error: If this error occurs, simply use `adctrl` to restart the worker on the current machine.

Error message: Patch not applied successfully, `adpatch` did not cleanup its restart files (*rf9).

Resolution to error: If this error occurs, execute the following as the instance owner:

```
$cd $APPL_TOP/admin/$CONTEXT_NAME
$mv restart restart_old
$mkdir restart
```

After cleaning up the restart files, you may then restart the `adpatch` session using `adpatch`.

Error message: ERROR: Javakey subcommand exited with status 1

Resolution to error: If this error occurs, the identity.obj file needs to be re-created. See Chapter 2 for steps to recreate the identity.obj file. Then, use adctrl to restart the failed worker.

Error message: No error message is displayed; rather the worker log file states that the worker is complete, yet adctrl indicates that the worker is still running.

Resolution to error: This patching problem occurs when the worker is complete, but did not update patching tables correctly to notify the adpatch session that it has finished. In this scenario, the adpatch session is still waiting for the finish return code from the worker. When this occurs, use adctrl to fail the worker, then restart the worker.

■**Tip** Any form, library, or report that fails to generate during the patch process can be regenerated manually after all patching and post-patching steps have completed. If the object still fails to compile, open an SR.

Additional Tips for Resolving Patching Issues

If a patch has hung or workers have failed, and the reason for this failure cannot be determined, it is advisable to check the number of invalid objects in the database. If the number of invalid objects is high, recompile the invalid objects in parallel and restart the patching session.

If the adpatch session is hung, and all other methods for resolution have been executed, it may be necessary to bounce the database and restart the patch session. This method for resolving patching issues is sometimes necessary, especially when applying large patches, such as Maintenance Packs.

If a failure occurs during the application of a patch, it may be necessary to apply another patch to resolve the issue. If this type of issue occurs during the application of a large patch, you may want to be able to restart the original patch from the point of failure. MetaLink Note 175485.1 provides details for applying a patch with adpatch already running.

Post-Patching Steps

Many patches require post-patching steps to be executed to complete the patching process. Also, if the patch was applied using options such as nocompiledb, notautoconfig, nogenerateportion, and others, those steps need to be performed now. Typical post-patching steps include generating message files, regenerating JAR files, regenerating menu options, relinking executables, recompiling invalids, and recompiling flexfields. Most of the post-patching requirements can be performed with the AD Administration utility, adadmin.

When executing the adadmin utility, you will be prompted with several questions. These include validating the APPL_TOP and database, entering the apps and system password, and validating the utility's environment settings, such as log filename. These variables can be set in an input parameter file to make manual responses to the questions unnecessary. This is similar to the steps required for adpatch.

As with other AD utilities, the menu options for the AD Administration utility may vary depending upon the AD patch level in the instance. The menu options for Minipack AD.I are shown in Figure 5-9.

```
        AD Administration Main Menu
-----------------------------------------------------

1.    Generate Applications Files menu

2.    Maintain Applications Files menu

3.    Compile/Reload Applications Database Entities menu

4.    Maintain Applications Database Entities menu

5.    Change Maintenance Mode

6.    Exit AD Administration
```

Figure 5-9. *The AD Administration Main Menu*

From the main menu, select the appropriate item to view its submenu. For example, to perform the post-patching steps of generating message files and product JAR files, select option 1 from the main menu, and select options 1 and 5 from the Generate Applications Files submenu shown in Figure 5-10.

```
        Generate Applications Files
-----------------------------------------

1.    Generate message files

2.    Generate form files

3.    Generate report files

4.    Generate graphics files

5.    Generate product JAR files

6.    Return to Main Menu
```

Figure 5-10. *The Generate Applications Files submenu*

Other common post-patching steps include recompiling database objects owned by apps and recompiling flexfields. These options are located in other submenus in adadmin. As an Applications DBA, you should be familiar with the menu options available from this utility.

■**Note** After the patches have completed, check for additional entries in the dba_jobs table. Verify that any newly created jobs are required by your environment.

Patching Cleanup

After a patch has completed, there will be an increase in the used space for the Oracle Applications filesystem. Some of this space can be reclaimed by removing backup copies of application code. For example, located in the $FND_TOP/bin directory are files such as FNDSCH.sav and FNDSCH.xxxxx, where xxxx is a number. These files are copies of the FNDSCH file created by the patch utility.

A list of directories containing backup files can be created using the UNIX find command. From the $APPL_TOP directory, execute the following command to list the directories containing *.sav files:

```
$find . -name "*.sav"
```

Those directories will also contain files with numbered extensions. These files can safely be removed from the system.

If there are any concerns about the removal of such files, create a temporary directory and move the files from their $[module]_TOP/bin location. After verifying that the system functions properly, these files can be removed.

Another area of cleanup involves the backup subdirectory of the directory where the patch was unbundled. If you are applying a patch from a common directory to multiple instances, space can be reclaimed in the patch directory by removing files written to the backup subdirectory from previous patch applications.

Database Patching

Database patching consists of either upgrades or interim fixes. Database upgrades are typically complex in nature and require installation of new software when upgrading from one point release to another. Obsolete and new initialization parameters must be reviewed when upgrading to a new release of the database.

Database upgrades can be accomplished manually or by using dbmig, the database migration utility. Since the method for upgrading the database is version and platform dependent, the associated readme file for the upgrade must be reviewed, and the steps required to perform the upgrade should be documented.

Interim patch fixes for the database are applied as the owner of the database install with the opatch utility or by running an operating system script. Details on how to apply database patches are outlined in the patch's readme.

Before upgrading or applying a patch to the database, the oraInst.loc file must point to the correct Oracle inventory location for the database ORACLE_HOME. It is also important to cleanly shut down the database before proceeding, and to perform a cold database backup.

The opatch utility is downloaded from MetaLink as patch number 2617419. The opatch utility requires Perl and JDK to function, and they must be installed and specified in the path and library environment variables. Once the opatch utility has been downloaded and unbundled, the Opatch directory of the opatch unbundled patch should be added to the PATH, as in the following example:

```
$export PATH=$PATH:/[path_of_2617419]/Opatch
```

The library path of Perl must also be specified with the following PERL5LIB environment variable, as in the following example:

```
$export PERL5LIB=[path_of_PERL]/lib
```

To validate that opatch is functioning properly, execute the following command with the lsinventory option:

```
$opatch lsinventory
```

Once opatch has been successfully set up, the database interim patch fix may be applied. To do this, first review the readme file for the patch. Make certain that all prerequisites have been met. Document any post-patching steps that are required. Download the patch and unbundle it. Change to the directory where the patch has been unbundled. Verify that the database has been shut down. Apply the patch by executing opatch as the database owner with the apply parameter, as in the following example:

```
$opatch apply
```

To verify that a patch has successfully been applied, the lsinventory option can again be executed. This will display all patches that have been applied to the database.

■**Note** If the `opatch` fails, there may be a `patch_locked` file located under the hidden directory `$ORACLE_HOME/.patch_storage`. The `opatch` utility may not be executed until the `patch_locked` file is removed.

Patching Best Practices

A proactive approach to patching is highly recommended. Patch fixes and upgrades will not only provide new functionality, but will also fix bugs for issues that may only come to light at the least opportune time. It is advisable to apply Maintenance Pack upgrades routinely and to not fall more than two point releases behind the most current release available. An automated approach to testing will facilitate patching efforts.

Oracle releases critical patches on a quarterly release schedule. The patches released are typically applicable to both the 11*i* Applications Technology Stack and supported Oracle RDBMS software. It is advisable to download and apply these patches on a scheduled basis, as they will primarily address security risks and Sarbanes-Oxley compliancy.

Technology stack components and product groups such as AD and FND are often prerequisites for future patches, such as Maintenance Packs and mandatory Family Packs. Therefore, it is important to stay current on these items. By applying such upgrades on a proactive basis, the time requirements for later patch sets may be greatly reduced.

Oracle often releases cumulative updates (CUs) or rollup patches (RUPs) for large patches, such as Maintenance Packs and Family Packs. Cumulative updates or rollup patches contain a collection of one-off patches that resolve errors resulting from the larger patch sets. When performing large patching efforts, it is recommended that you download and apply the latest cumulative update available for your environment.

■ ■ ■

## CHAPTER 6

Toolkit

In order to manage Oracle Applications, it is a good idea for every Oracle Applications DBA to develop a toolkit. An Applications DBA's toolkit is a source for commands, utilities, and scripts that can be executed to find information or implement tasks in a speedy fashion. All of the scripts and tips provided thus far in this guide are part of your toolkit. This chapter will provide additional toolkit information on the following topics:

- **Oracle Applications utilities and commands**: Many Oracle Applications utilities and commands have already been discussed in this guide; however, there are still some that are required for the day-to-day management of the system. This section will look at additional commands that are used to administer the E-Business Suite.

- **Application component versions**: An Oracle Applications DBA is often required to determine versions for the different components of the Oracle E-Business Suite. This information may assist with patching requirements, be provided to Oracle Support, or be used to troubleshoot an issue. This section will outline the methods for obtaining application component version information.

- **Useful UNIX commands and usage tips**: In addition to the UNIX commands already described in this guide, there are still many that are helpful to an Oracle Applications DBA. This section will describe and outline the syntax of useful UNIX commands.

- **Scheduled jobs and scripts**: Performing proactive maintenance is a must for an Oracle Applications DBA. This section will offer tips for scheduling jobs and scripts using `crontab` and other scheduling tools.

- **Preventative maintenance**: Routinely performing certain tasks can make the difference between a system running and performing as expected or running poorly. It is critical for the overall health of Oracle Applications for certain tasks to be executed on a scheduled basis. This section will describe preventative maintenance tasks that should be performed periodically.

- **Application instance clones**: Copies of the production Oracle Applications is often required for development and testing purposes. This is achieved by performing a *clone*. This section will outline cloning documentation and requirements.

A toolkit is a dynamic library that will continue to evolve with an Applications DBA's environment and as new versions and upgrades are developed by Oracle. It is important to manage and update your toolkit on a regular basis.

Oracle Applications Utilities and Commands

We have covered numerous Oracle Applications utilities and commands, but there are still a number of them that need to be discussed in order to successfully administer the E-Business Suite:

- Application component startup and shutdown scripts
- Changing application passwords
- Relinking application executables
- Regenerating forms, libraries, and menus
- Recompiling JSP pages

Application Component Startup and Shutdown Scripts

Each component of the Oracle E-Business Suite has a corresponding script that can be used to start, stop, and in some cases query the status of the component. All log files for the scripts are located in the $COMMON_TOP/admin/log/$CONTEXT_NAME directory. These scripts are listed and described in Table 6-1.

Table 6-1. *Application Component Startup and Shutdown Script Files*

Script	Parameters	Component Description	Log File
adapcctl.sh	[start|stop|status]	Apache Web Server Listener	adapcctl.txt
adaprstctl.sh	[start|stop|status]	Apache Web Server Listener in restricted mode	adapcctl.txt
adcmctl.sh	[start|stop|abort|status] [apps user]/[apps password]	Concurrent Manager	adcmctl.txt
adfrmctl.sh	[start|stop|status]	Forms Server Listener	f60svrm.txt
adalnctl.sh	[start|stop|status] [listener_name]	Applications RPC Listener	adalnctl.txt
gsmstart.sh		Start FNDSM, which is referenced in the listener.ora file. This script is not executed directly, but is called by the adalnctl.sh script.	
adtcfctl.sh	[start|stop|status]	TCF Socket Server	adtcfctl.txt
addisctl.sh	[start|stop|status]	Discoverer	addisctl.txt
adfmsctl.sh	[start|stop|status]	Forms Metrics Server	adfmsctl.txt
adfmcctl.sh	[start|stop|status]	Forms Metrics Client	adfmcctl.txt
adrepctl.sh	[start|stop|status]	Reports Server	rep60_CONTEXT_NAME.txt
jtffmctl.sh	[start|stop]	Fulfillment Server process	jtffmctl.txt
adstpall.sh	None	Stop APPL_TOP Server processes	date+mdhm.log
adstrtal.sh	None	Start APPL_TOP Server processes	date+mdhm.log

■**Tip** Since the directory where the startup/shutdown scripts are located is navigated to so frequently, an environment variable may be set in order to ease navigation to this directory. For example: `$SCRIPT_TOP=$APPLCOMN/admin/scripts/$CONTEXT_NAME`.

To use the component startup/shutdown scripts, log in to the server as the instance owner, and execute the command with the parameter to start, stop, or check the status of the component. The following is an example of starting the Forms Server as the VIS instance owner:

```
$su - vis
$cd $SCRIPT_TOP
$./adfrmctl.sh start
```

The `adstpall.sh` and `adstrtal.sh` scripts are used to start each component of the application, and they can be copied and customized to start only the components that are relevant to your environment. For example, you may not require the Forms Metrics Server and Forms Metrics Client processes; these scripts can be removed from custom startup and shutdown scripts. The following is an example of a custom start script that will start the Apache Server, RPC Listener, Concurrent Manager, and Forms Server:

```
#Custom startup script
$SCRIPT_TOP/adapcctl.sh start
$SCRIPT_TOP/adalnctl.sh start
$SCRIPT_TOP/adcmctl.sh start APPS/APPS
$SCRIPT_TOP/adfrmctl.sh start
#End of custom startup script
```

This script assumes both the APPS user and password are APPS.

Changing Application, Oracle, and the APPLSYS/APPS Passwords

An *application user* is a user that is defined in the E-Business Suite. For example, an AP Specialist using Oracle Financials is defined as an application user. An Oracle user is a database user only and is a schema owner of modules that are used in the application; for example, AP, GL, and BEN. At times it is necessary to change passwords for application users, Oracle users, or the APPS and APPLSYS passwords.

Changing an Application User's Password

An application user's password can be changed via the application or with the FNDCPASS utility. To change a user's password in the application, log in to the application and navigate to the Define User screen (shown in Figure 6-1) by selecting Security ➤ Define ➤ User. Query for the user in question, type in a new password twice, and save the form. The password will have to conform to the rules set with profile options Sign%.

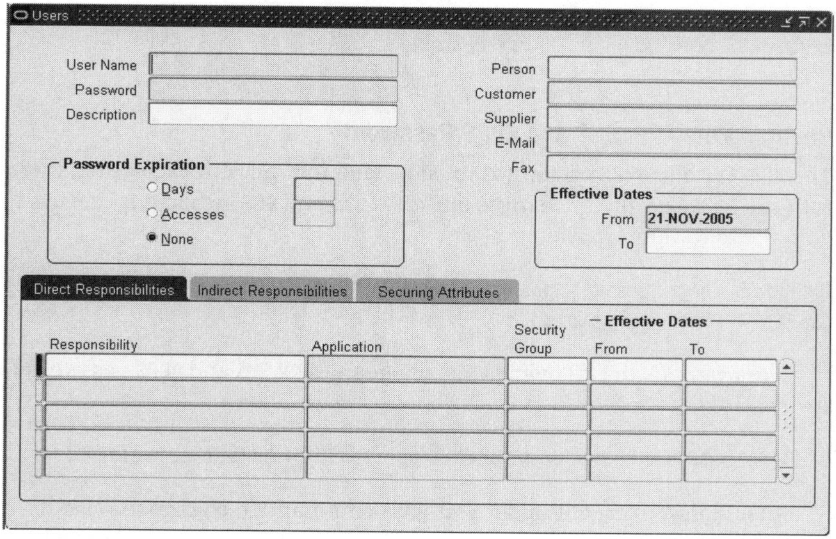

Figure 6-1. *Resetting an application user's password with the Define User functionality*

A faster method for changing an application user's password is to use the FNDCPASS utility located on the Admin Node. To change the password of a user in the application, the following parameters are used with FNDCPASS:

```
FNDCPASS [apps_user]/[apps_passwd] O Y system/[passwd] USER ➥
[user_name] [password]
```

For example, the following command will change user grudd's password to passwd#1:

```
$FNDCPASS APPS/APPS O Y system/manager USER grudd passwd#1
```

Changing an Oracle User's Password

To change the password of an Oracle user, the following parameters are used
with FNDCPASS:

```
FNDCPASS [apps_user]/[apps_passwd] O Y system/[passwd] ORACLE ➡
[user_name] [password]
```

For example, the following command will change application schema
AP's password to passwd#1:

```
$FNDCPASS APPS/APPS O Y system/manager ORACLE AP passwd#1
```

Changing the APPLSYS and APPS Password

The APPLSYS and APPS passwords must be kept in sync with each other; therefore, the FNDCPASS utility changes both APPLSYS and APPS when it is executed
with the following parameters:

```
FNDCPASS [apps_user]/[apps_passwd] O Y system/[passwd] ➡
SYSTEM APPLSYS [password]
```

For example, the following will change the APPLSYS and APPS passwords
to oracle#1:

```
$FNDCPASS APPS/APPS O Y system/manager SYSTEM APPLSYS oracle#1
```

In addition to executing the FNDCPASS command to change the APPS
password, the autoconfig utility must be run or the APPS password must be
manually changed in the following files:

- $ORACLE_HOME/listener/cfg/wdbsvr.app
- adcmctl.sh
- $OA_HTML/bin/appsweb.cfg
- $AD_TOP/admin/template/CGIcmd.dat (if in use)

■**Note** When changing the different types of user passwords with FNDCPASS, the primary difference is the use of the USER, ORACLE, or SYSTEM parameter. The USER
parameter is for application users. The ORACLE parameter is used for Oracle schema
owners. The SYSTEM parameter is for changing the APPLSYS and APPS passwords.

If you are running a minimum of Oracle Applications 11.5.10 and Apache 1.3.12, it is also possible to encrypt the APPS password in the wdbsvr.app file. The steps for doing so are as follows:

1. Set the following in the wdbsvr.app file: `administrators = all`
2. Comment out the following in the wdbsvr.app file: `custom_auth`
3. Restart the HTTP Server.
4. Go to the following URL:
   `http://[hostname.domain.com]:[port]/pls/admin/gateway.html`
5. Edit the Applications DAD by entering the new APPS password.
6. Save the configuration. The password in the wdbsvr.app file is now encrypted.
7. Set the following in the wdbsvr.app file: `administrators=system`
8. Set the following in the wdbsvr.app file: `custom_auth=CUSTOM`

Tip After changing the APPS password, it is advisable to verify that the FNDCPASS command has executed properly and that Oracle Applications functions normally. Review the log file generated by FNDCPASS and, if necessary, correct any errors. Then, log in to the database and application. These steps provide a quick test of the APPS password change.

Relinking Application Executables

At times, it is necessary to relink executables for the application. This requirement occurs for many reasons, including post-patching steps and resolving application execution issues. The AD Admin utility may be used to relink all application executables. Additionally, the AD Relink utility may be used to relink AD executable programs with the Oracle Server product libraries. This section will cover both these topics.

Using AD Relink to Relink AD Executables

The AD Relink utility may be used to relink AD executable programs. The syntax of the adrelink.sh command is as follows:

```
adrelink.sh force={y|n} [<optional args>] "<targets>"
```

or

```
adrelink.sh force={y|n} [<optional args>] filelist=<file>
```

In both cases, "`<targets>`" is "`<product> <module name>`", and `<file>` is the name of a file that contains a list of files to relink. Valid `<optional args>` values for `adrelink.sh` are listed in Table 6-2.

Table 6-2. *Description and Values for* `<optional_args>` *with* `adrelink.sh`

`<optional args>`	**Values**	**Description**
force	[y|n]	This option specifies whether the relink should be forced, meaning relink is not optional.
envfile	[adsetenv.sh]	This option is only used by the adsetup script.
link_debug	[y|n]	This option specifies whether the relink is done with or without debugging. The default value is n.
backup_mode	[none|all|file]	This option specifies whether a backup should be made when executing a forced relink; none means no files will be backed up, all means all files will be backed up, and file means files listed in the $APPL_TOP/admin/ adlinkbk.txt file will be backed up.

The following is an example of using `adrelink.sh` to force relink the adadmin module:

`$adrelink.sh force=y "ad adadmin"`

The following is an example of using `adrelink.sh` to force relink the adadmin and adpatch modules:

`$adrelink.sh force=y "ad adadmin""ad adpatch"`

The following is an example of using `adrelink.sh` to force relink all AD executables:

`$adrelink.sh force=y "ad all"`

Using AD Admin to Relink Application Executables

AD Admin also provides the ability to relink application executables. From the Maintain Application Files menu, select the option to Relink Application Programs. This program will require you to respond to the following questions:

Question: Do you wish to proceed with the relink [Yes]?

Recommended response: Press the Enter key or type **Yes** to proceed with the relink; otherwise, type **No**.

Question: Enter list of products to link [all]

Recommended response: This option gives you the opportunity to narrow the scope of the relink; for example, you may want to limit the recompile to AD products. Press Enter or type **all** if you want to generate all products; otherwise type the products to relink.

Question: Relink with debug information [no]

Recommended response: Press Enter or type **No** if you do not want to relink with debugging information; otherwise, type **Yes**. It is helpful to relink with debugging information if you are experiencing errors during the relink process.

Regenerating Forms, Libraries, and Menus

At times it is necessary to regenerate forms, libraries, or menus to fix issues with them, to synchronize the generated object with the underlying database object, or as a post-patching step. This section will cover regenerating forms, libraries, and menus by using f60gen and AD Admin.

Using f60gen

The f60gen utility can be used to manually regenerate forms, libraries, and menus. The syntax for the f60gen command is as follows:

```
f60gen [filename.[fmb|mmb|pll]] module_type=[form|menu|library] \
output_file=[path/file_name].[fmx|mmx|plx] \
userid=[apps]/[apps_password]
```

Required parameters for the f60gen command are described in Table 6-3.

Table 6-3. *Required Parameters for the* f60gen *Command*

Parameter	Parameter Values	Description
module	[filename.[fmb|mmb|pll]]	Source file for the form, menu, or library file to be regenerated; extensions are .fmb for forms, .mmb for menus, and .pll for libraries
module_type	[form|menu|library]	Parameter that instructs f60gen which type of object is being generated
output_file	[path/file_name].[fmx|mmx|plx]	Parameter that identifies the location, name, and extension of the generated file; extensions are .fmx for forms, .mmx for menus, and .plx for libraries
userid	[apps]/[apps_password]	Name of the APPS user and the APPS user password

The following is an example of using f60gen to generate the GLXJIRUN.fmb form:

```
$cd $AU_TOP/forms/US
$f60gen module=GLXJIRUN.fmb module_type=form \
output_file=$GL_TOP/forms/US/GLXJIRUN.fmx userid=APPS/APPS
```

■Tip Prior to generating the form, menu, or library, you should locate the source and generated files using the UNIX find command.

Using AD Admin to Regenerate Forms, Libraries, and Menus

AD Admin provides a menu for regenerating forms, libraries, and menus. There are many options associated with this menu selection, so only an overview of using the menu will be provided here.

To regenerate forms, you should start an AD Admin session and select the following menu options: Generate Applications Files Menu ➤ Generate Forms Files. The following is an example of some of the options you have when using AD Admin to regenerate forms, menus, or libraries:

Question: Do you want to regenerate Oracle Forms PL/SQL library files [Yes]?

Recommended response: Press the Enter key or type **Yes** to regenerate Forms PL/SQL libraries; otherwise, type **No**.

Question: Do you want to regenerate Oracle Forms menu files [Yes]?

Recommended response: Press the Enter key or type **Yes** to regenerate Forms menu files; otherwise, type **No**.

Question: Do you want to regenerate Oracle Forms executable files [Yes]?

Recommended response: Press the Enter key or type **Yes** to regenerate Forms executable files; otherwise, type **No**.

Question: Enter list of products ('all' for all products) [all]

Recommended response: This option gives you the opportunity to narrow the scope of the recompile; for example, you may want to limit the recompile to GL products. Press Enter or type **all** if you want to generate all products; otherwise type the product module, such as **GL**, **AP**, or **BEN**.

Question: Generate specific Forms objects for each selected product [No]?

Recommended response: This option gives you the opportunity to further reduce the scope of the recompile, by limiting the form, library, or menu to be recompiled. Press Enter or type **No** if you want to generate all forms, libraries, and menus for a specific product; otherwise type **Yes**, and a list of forms, libraries, and menus will be displayed. You will then be able to choose from this list of objects.

Recompiling JSP Pages

JSP pages automatically compile upon access; however, performance may be improved if the JSP pages are manually recompiled. Recompiling is accomplished by using the JSP precompiler.

Prerequisites and requirements for using the JSP precompiler are outlined in MetaLink Note 215268.1. The JSP precompiler is invoked using the `ojspCompile.pl` Perl script. The syntax of using the precompiler is as follows:

```
ojspCompile.pl [COMMAND] [ARGS]
```

Key options for the [COMMAND] parameter are outlined in Table 6-4. Key options for the [ARGS] parameter are outlined in Table 6-5.

Table 6-4. [COMMAND] *Parameter Options for* ojspCompile.pl

[COMMAND] **Parameter**	**Description**
--compile	Update the dependency and compile the delta
-out <file>	Update the dependency and output the delta to the file

Table 6-5. [ARGS] *Parameter Options for* ojspCompile.pl

[ARGS] **Parameter**	**Description**
-s <regex>	Search for condition in JSP filename; for example: -s 'jtf%'
-p <procs>	Specify the number of parallel executions
-log <file>	Specify the name of the log file
--flush	Force all parent JSP pages to be recompiled

The following is an example of force compiling all JSP pages with parallel execution of 10:

```
$ojspCompile.pl --compile --flush -p 10
```

The following is an example of compiling all delta JSP pages:

```
$ojspCompile.pl --compile -log /oracle/admin/vis/log/compile_jsps.log
```

The following is an example of compiling all JSPs that start with the string jtf:

```
$ojspCompile.pl --compile -s 'jtf%'
```

Determining Component Versions

Determining versions of the different components is useful for researching functionality, issues, certification levels, patching requirements, and providing information to Oracle Support. This section provides information for obtaining version information for the following components:

- Application file versions
- JInitiator version
- Apache version and rollup patch
- Forms and PL/SQL version
- Framework version
- OJSP version
- JDK version
- Java class file version
- Database version

Identifying Application File Versions

Often you will be required to identify the version of application files. Application file versions can be obtained with the `ident` or `adident` commands or the `strings` command. This section will outline how to use each of these commands to obtain application version information.

Using ident or adident

The `ident` command is available for most flavors of UNIX; exceptions are SUN and AIX. For SUN and AIX, the `adident` command is used.

The syntax for both `ident` and `adident` is as follows:

```
[ident|adident] [pattern] [file1 |, file2, file3, . . .]
```

In this statement, `[pattern]` is the identifying pattern that is being searched for in the file, and `[file1 |, file2, file3, . . .]` is the list of files being reviewed.

Here is an example:

```
$ident Header OA.jsp
```

```
OA.jsp:
$Header OA.jsp 115.56 2004/07/16 04:02:21 atgops1 noship $
```

Using the strings Command

The `strings` command may also be used to retrieve file version information. The syntax for the `strings` command is as follows:

```
$strings -a [filename] | grep [pattern]
```

In this statement, [filename] is the name of the file being reviewed, and [pattern] is the pattern being searched for in the file.

Here is an example:

```
$strings -a OA.jsp | grep Header
```

```
<%! public static final String RCS_ID = "$Header: OA.jsp 115.56
2004/07/16 04:02
:21 atgops1 noship $"; %>
```

JInitiator Version

When determining JInitiator versions, there are two components to consider: the application and the client. To determine which version of JInitiator the application is configured to use, review the $OA_HTML/bin/ appsweb_${CONTEXT_NAME}.cfg file. This file contains information regarding the version of JInitiator for the application, as seen in this example:

```
; JInitiator Parameters
; ---------------------
; The following parameters relate to the version of JInitiator.
; !!! IMPORTANT !!!
; When patching this file, you must update these parameters to ➥
reflect
; the JInitiator version you are using in you environment. Follow
; Metalink Apps11i Alert "Upgrading the JInitiator version used with
; Oracle Applications 11i" (Note:124606.1)
jinit_ver_name=Version=1,3,1,23
jinit_mimetype=application/x-jinit-applet;version=1.3.1.23
```

To determine which version of JInitiator the client is using, you should enable the Oracle JInitiator's Java Console. (Additional details for enabling the Java Console were provided in Chapter 3 of this guide.) Log in to Oracle Applications and go to a Forms responsibility to start JInitiator. Reviewing the contents of the Java Console will display the version of JInitiator that is being used by the client, as shown in Figure 6-2.

■**Caution** The JInitiator version used by the application and the client must match. If the client does not have the correct version installed, there may be an issue with the ability of the user to download and install JInitiator. In order to resolve JInitiator installation issues, please see Chapter 3 of this guide.

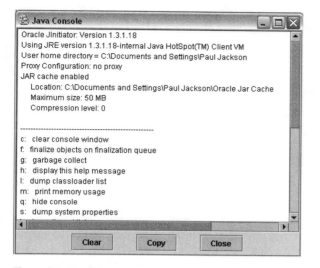

Figure 6-2. *JInitiator version for Oracle Applications as displayed in the Java Console*

Apache Version and Rollup Patch

Apache version and rollup patch information may be obtained on the Web Node by executing the httpd -version command. Here is an example:

```
$cd $APACHE_TOP/Apache/bin/
$httpd -version
```

```
Server version: Oracle HTTP Server Powered by Apache/1.3.1.19 (Unix)
Server built:   Oct 7 2003 18:00:36 (iAS 1.0.2.2.2 rollup 4)
```

Forms and PL/SQL Version

Forms version information may be obtained on the Forms Node or in the About menu of a Forms client session. To obtain version information from the Forms Node, execute the f60gen command with the help=y parameter. Here is an example:

```
$f60gen help=y
```

Forms 6.0 (Form Compiler) Version 6.0.8.25.2 (Production)

Forms 6.0 (Form Compiler): Release - Production

(c) Copyright 1999 Oracle Corporation. All rights reserved.

PL/SQL Version 8.0.6.3.0 (Production)

To obtain the version information from a Forms client session, click on the Help ➤ About menu. This will display the About dialog box. In the About dialog box, scroll to the Forms version information, as displayed in Figure 6-3.

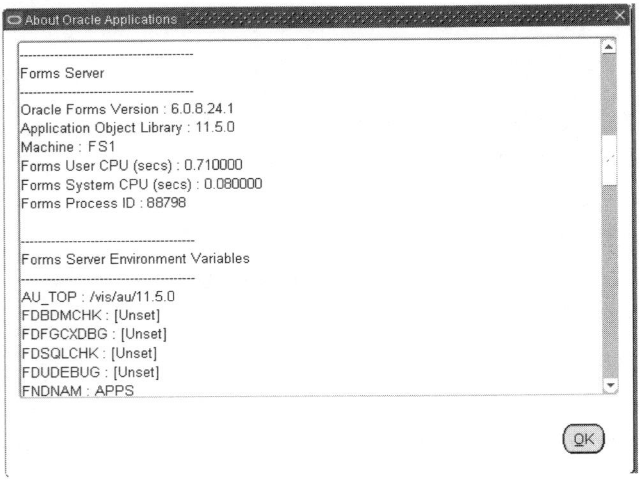

Figure 6-3. *Forms About dialog box showing Forms version information*

The results obtained for Forms version information can be used to look up the Forms patchset, as shown in Table 6-6. Additional information regarding Forms patchset versions may be obtained in MetaLink Note 266541.1.

Table 6-6. *Forms Patchset and Version Information*

Forms Patchset	Forms Version
17	6.0.8.26
16	6.0.8.25
15	6.0.8.24
14	6.0.8.23

Oracle Applications Framework Version

Oracle Applications (OA) Framework version information may be obtained by using the ident, adident, or strings command to retrieve header information from the OA.jsp file in the $OA_HTML and $FND_TOP/html directories. The following commands are executed to retrieve OA.jsp version information:

```
$ident Header $FND_TOP/html/OA.jsp
```

```
$Header OA.jsp 115.56 2004/07/16 04:02:21 atgops1 noship $
```

```
$ident Header $OA_HTML/OA.jsp
```

```
$Header OA.jsp 115.56 2004/07/16 04:02:21 atgops1 noship $
```

Header information is then used to look up the corresponding OA Framework version, as shown in Table 6-7. MetaLink Note 275874.1 can be used to retrieve additional OA Framework version information.

Table 6-7. *OA Framework and* OA.jsp *Version*

OA Framework Version	OA.jsp Version
5.10	115.56
5.7	115.36
5.6	115.27

The OA Framework version can also be determined by accessing the following URL in your web browser: http://[hostname.domain.com]:[port]/OA_HTML/OAInfo.jsp

OJSP Version

OJSP version information can be obtained by setting up a test JSP file. With a text editor, create the test.jsp file in the $OA_HTML directory. The contents of the test.jsp file should be as follows:

```
<%=application getAttribute("oracle.jsp.versionNumber")%>
```

To retrieve the OJSP version, access test.jsp from a web browser using the following URL: http://[hostname.domain.com]:[port]/OA_HTML/test.jsp. The resulting page in the browser will display the OJSP version.

JDK Version

JDK version information can be retrieved using several commands from the UNIX prompt. The java -version command may be used as the instance owner from the command line to determine the default JDK version being set for the environment. Here is an example:

```
$which java
```

```
/usr/java/1.5.0
```

```
$java -version
```

```
java version "1.5.0"
```

Additionally, ADJVAPRG, CLASSPATH, AFJVAPRG, and AF_CLASSPATH must be checked to determine the JDK version being used by the various application components:

```
$ADJVAPRG -version
$echo $CLASSPATH
$AFJVAPRG -version
$echo $AF_CLASSPATH                          .
```

The results of the ADJVAPRG -version and AFJVAPRG -version commands should resolve to J2SE "1.x.x.x", as in the following example:

```
java version "1.5.0.0"
```

The CLASSPATH and the AF_CLASSPATH environment variables should contain the JDK_TOP path set to the version of JDK implemented. Also, at a minimum, the following JAR files must be included in both the CLASSPATH and the AF_CLASSPATH:

- [JDK_TOP]/lib/dt.jar
- [JDK_TOP]/lib/tools.jar
- [JDK_TOP]/jre/lib/rt.jar
- [JDK_TOP]/jre/lib/charsets.jar

For example, when JDK_TOP is equal to /usr/java/1.5.0, the echo $CLASSPATH and echo $AF_CLASSPATH commands would include the following:

- /usr/java/1.5.0/lib/dt.jar
- /usr/java/1.5.0/lib/tools.jar
- /usr/java/1.5.0/jre/lib/rt.jar
- /usr/java/1.5.0/jre/lib/charsets.jar

Java Class File Versions

Class file versions may be obtained from the apps.zip file or the class file. Which method is used depends upon whether the environment has migrated to the apps.zip file per MetaLink Note 220188.1. To obtain Java class file version information, a combination of the unzip and grep commands, followed by a combination of the strings and grep commands are used.

The steps to retrieve version information for a Java class from the apps.zip file are as follows:

1. Review the zip file to obtain the full path of the zipped Java class:

   unzip -l apps.zip | grep [class file]

2. Extract the Java class from the zipped file:

   unzip -j apps.zip [path/class file]

   where [path/class file] is the path for the class filename retrieved from step 1.

3. Retrieve the header information from the Java class with the strings command:

   strings -a [class file] | grep Header

   where [class file] is the path for the class filename retrieved from step 1.

If the apps.zip file is not in use, the class file version may be obtained by using the strings command. For example, to retrieve the file version information for MOLine.class located in the $JAVA_TOP/oracle/apps/inv/mo/ server directory, use this command:

```
$strings -a $JAVA_TOP/oracle/apps/inv/mo/server/MOLine.class \
| grep '$Header'
```

```
H$Header: MOLine.java 115.36.115100.2 2004/11/18 22:51:49 vipathak
ship $
```

■Note Step 2 in the preceding list extracts the class file to the directory where the unzip command is executed. You should delete the extracted class file once version information has been retrieved in step 3.

Database Version Query

The version of the database may be obtained simply by reviewing the banner that is displayed when connecting to the instance via SQL*Plus on the database server. Here's an example:

```
$sqlplus
```

```
SQL*Plus: Release 9.2.0.5.0 - Production on Sat Nov 19 16:31:01 2005

Copyright (c) 1982, 2002, Oracle Corporation.  All rights reserved.

Enter user-name: sys as sysdba
Enter password:

Connected to:
Oracle9i Enterprise Edition Release 9.2.0.5.0 - 64bit Production
With the Partitioning option
JServer Release 9.2.0.5.0 - Production
```

Additional information regarding the database component installations and versions may be obtained by executing the following query:

```
SQL> select comp_name, version, status
  2    from dba_registry;
```

COMP_NAME	VERSION	STATUS
Oracle9i Catalog Views	9.2.0.5.0	VALID
Oracle9i Packages and Types	9.2.0.5.0	VALID
JServer JAVA Virtual Machine	9.2.0.5.0	VALID
Oracle9i Java Packages	9.2.0.5.0	VALID
Oracle XDK for Java	9.2.0.7.0	VALID
Oracle Text	9.2.0.5.0	VALID
Oracle9i Real Application Clusters	9.2.0.5.0	INVALID

```
Spatial                      9.2.0.5.0          VALID
Oracle interMedia            9.2.0.5.0          VALID
Oracle XML Database          9.2.0.5.0          INVALID
```

Additional Commands and Usage Tips

Many UNIX commands and SQL scripts have been reviewed and used thus far in this guide. However, there are many more that are used frequently in the day-to-day management of the Oracle E-Business Suite. This guide will cover some additional common UNIX commands and usage tips.

This section will start with some general tips and then cover the following specific topics:

- Using chown, chmod, kill, find, df, du, and tar
- Finding and removing memory segments and semaphores with ipcs and ipcrm
- Finding and removing print jobs with lpstat and lpqrm
- Removing a database session and server process

■**Tip** An Applications DBA supporting Oracle on a UNIX-based system should consider investing in additional reference material specific to UNIX.

General Tips

Prior to discussing additional UNIX commands, it is important to cover some UNIX basics.

First, there are many options available for finding help on a specific command—we will present three alternatives. Your system may have the manual (man) pages installed—this tool can provide detailed descriptions of commands. The syntax for the man command is as follows:

```
man [command]
```

Here is an example that looks up the man pages for df:

```
$man df
```

Another option is to use quick help for a command—if the manual pages are not installed in your system, this may be the only available option from the server. It can be accomplished by using the -? parameter with the command. The syntax for this help feature is as follows:

```
[command] -?
```

Here is an example:

```
$df -?
```

Lastly, it is possible to get information about commands by using web search engines. These sites, like Google and Yahoo, may direct you to online versions of manual pages for UNIX commands.

After you develop an understanding for the syntax of a command, you can look for opportunities to use the commands to their fullest potential. One way to accomplish that is to combine the command with other UNIX commands. The pipe character (|) will allow multiple commands to be run together. An example of this is to use the grep command to find information about a specific process ID, such as 2342:

```
$ps -ef | grep 2342
```

Using chown

The UNIX chown command is used to change ownership of a UNIX file. There are many optional parameters that can be used with the chown command, but only a few parameters will be discussed in this section. The parameters are described in Table 6-8.

You are required to execute the chown command as the root user or the file owner. The basic syntax of this command is as follows:

```
chown -[R][h] [user].[group] [directory|filename]
```

Table 6-8. *Parameters for* chown

Parameter	Description
[R]	Optional parameter used to recursively change ownership for directories and files in directories
[h]	Optional parameter used to change ownership of a symbolic link, but not the source of the link
[user]	Mandatory parameter that specifies the new owner of the file
[group]	Optional parameter that specifies the new group ownership
[directory|filename]	Mandatory parameter that specifies the name of the directory or file for which ownership is being changed

The following is an example of changing ownership of the ORACLE.env file to vis and group ownership to dba:

```
$ls -l ORACLE.env
```

```
-rw-rw-rw- root system ORACLE.env
```

```
$chown vis.dba ORACLE.env
$ls -ltr ORACLE.env
```

```
-rw-rw-rw- oracle dba ORACLE.env
```

The following is an example of recursively changing ownership of the /vis/oratop/iAS directory to vis and group ownership to dba:

```
$chown -Rh vis.dba /vis/oratop/iAS
```

■**Tip** It is recommended that you use the -h parameter with chown so that you do not affect ownership of the source of symbolic links.

Using chmod

The UNIX chmod command is used to change the permissions of a UNIX file. There are many optional parameters that can be used with the chmod command, but only a few parameters will be discussed in this section; these are described in Table 6-9. The basic syntax of this command is as follows:

```
chmod -[R] [u|g|o|a][+|-][r|w|x] [directory|filename]
```

Table 6-9. *Parameters for* chmod

Parameter	Description
[R]	Optional parameter used to recursively set permissions for directories and files in directories.
[u|g|o|a]	Mandatory parameter used to specify the setting of the permission for the u (user), the g (group), o (other), or a (all).
[+|-]	Mandatory parameter that specifies whether to grant (+) or remove (-) the permission.

Continued

Table 6-9. *Continued*

Parameter	Description
[r|w|x]	Mandatory parameter that specifies the permission being set: read (r), write (w), or execute (x).
[directory|filename]	Mandatory parameter that specifies the name of the directory or file for which ownership is being changed.

Here is an example of changing permissions of the restart_apache.sh file to grant execute permission to the dba group:

```
$ls -l restart_apache.sh
```

```
-rwxrw-rw- vis dba restart_apache.sh
```

```
$chmod g+x restart_apache.sh
$ls -ltr restart_apache.sh
```

```
-rwxrwxrw- vis dba restart_apache.sh
```

Additionally, a numeric description can be used to represent the binary value for read, write, and execute permissions for a file. This value can be assigned at the owner, group, and other levels. The available options are displayed in Table 6-10.

Table 6-10. *Numerical Values for File Permissions*

Numerical Value	Binary Value	Permissions
0	000	None
1	001	Execute
2	010	Write
3	011	Write, Execute
4	100	Read
5	101	Read, Execute
6	110	Read, Write
7	111	Read, Write, Execute

An example of changing permissions of the `restart_apache.sh` file to grant read, write, and execute permissions to the owner and group only is as follows:

```
$ls -l restart_apache.sh
```

```
-r-xrw-rw- vis dba restart_apache.sh
```

```
$chmod 770 restart_apache.sh
$ls -ltr restart_apache.sh
```

```
-rwxrwx--- vis dba restart_apache.sh
```

■**Note** For security reasons, it is common to set the other permissions to 0 in order to prevent access to files by system users who are not members of the appropriate security group.

Using kill

The UNIX `kill` command may be used to terminate a process on the server. First, the process ID must be obtained by using the `ps` command, and then the `kill` command can be executed.

The syntax for the `kill` command is as follows:

```
kill -[9] [process id]
```

In this command, [9] is an optional parameter used to force kill a process.

The following is an example of obtaining a process ID and issuing the `kill` command to terminate the process:

```
$ps -ef | grep f60webmx | grep vis
```

```
f60webmx 2899121 1 0 08:50:21 - 1:51 vis
```

```
$kill -9 2899121
```

Using find

The UNIX find command may be used to find files or directories on the server. As with the other UNIX commands that have been presented, there are many options available, but only basic syntax for the command will be given for finding files on the server:

```
find . -name "[filename]" -print
```

In this command, the period (.) means to begin searching in this directory and all subdirectories; [filename] is the name of the file or directory that the find command is locating. The asterisk (*) may be used as a wildcard character in the search.

The result of executing the find command is a list of the paths and files that match the criteria. Here is an example:

```
$cd /vis/oratop/iAS
$find . -name "*.env" -print
./ORACLE.env
./DB.env
```

With the find command, it is also possible to locate files based upon size, change date, and several other parameters. Familiarize yourself with these options.

Using df

The UNIX df command may be used to obtain filesystem space information. As with other UNIX commands, df has many parameter options, but the use of interest here is the df -m syntax. This will display block information for filesystems. Executing df -m is useful for determining the amount of free space in megabytes and assessing whether additional space is required.

Here is an example:

```
$df -m
```

Filesystem	1M-blocks	Used	Available	Use%	Mounted on
/dev/cciss/c0d0p3	66353	14375	48607	23%	/
/dev/cciss/c0d0p1	50	34	14	70%	/boot
none	1760	0	1760	0%	/dev/shm
sc:/u01	440507	154427	286080	36%	/d01/oracle
sc:/u04	440507	154427	286080	36%	➡
/d02/oracle/visappl					
sc:/u03	440507	154427	286080	36%	➡
/d02/oracle/viscomn					

```
sc:/u02                    440507    154427    286080   36% ➡
/d02/oracle/patches
```

Using du

The UNIX du command may be used to obtain filesystem space information. This command will return information on space usage by all subdirectories below the location the command was executed from.

Executing a sort command along with the du command is useful for determining which directories are using the most space. This information can help the Applications DBA resolve issues with space usage. Here is an example:

```
$du | sort -n
```

```
4        ./oraInventory/locks
12       ./.kde/Autostart
16       ./.kde
16       ./oraInventory/ContentsXML
36       ./oraInventory/logs
400      ./patches/3006092/sht/lib
404      ./patches/3006092/sht
428      ./patches/3006092
548      ./oraInventory/Contents
612      ./oraInventory
43860    ./patches/2837811/sht/lib
43864    ./patches/2837811/sht
43888    ./patches/2837811
124252   ./patches
127516   .
```

Using tar

Some of the most common uses of the UNIX tar command include archiving directories and files into one single file, extracting files and directories that have been archived with the tar command, and copying directories and files from one location to another. Parameters for the tar command are provided in Table 6-11.

The following `tar` syntax can be used to compress a directory and its contents:

```
tar -cvf [tar file name] [directory1 | file1 , directory2 ➥
| file2 ... directoryn | filen ]
```

The following `tar` syntax can be used to extract a tar file:

```
tar -xvf [tar file name]
```

Table 6-11. *Parameters for the* `tar` *Command*

Parameter	Description
[c|x]	Mandatory parameter used to create or extract an archive: c (create), x (extract)
[v]	Optional parameter used to verbosely list the processed files
[f]	Mandatory parameter used to specify the name of the file or directory to be archived or extracted
[directory]	Parameter that specifies the name of the directory that is to be archived or extracted
[tar file name]	Parameter that specifies the file that is being copied or extracted
[directoryn, filen]	Parameter that specifies the name of the directory that is to be archived

The following `tar` syntax can be used to copy a target directory and its contents from one directory to another on the same server:

```
(cd [source path] ; tar -cf - . ) | ( cd [target path] ; tar -xvf - )
```

The following example will copy the `/vis/oratop/iAS` directory to the `/newvis/oratop/iAS` directory:

```
$(cd /vis/oratop/iAS ; tar -cf - . ) | ( cd /newvis/oratop/iAS ; \
tar -xvf - )
```

Finding and Removing Memory Segments and Semaphores

Shared memory and semaphores being used on a UNIX server can be displayed and removed using the `ipcs` and `ipcrm` commands, respectively. These commands are useful when a stopped or killed process does not relinquish a shared memory segment or semaphore. This may become evident if you try to restart a process or try to execute an upgrade or patching step that finds the process is still holding a memory segment or semaphore.

This is an example of how to use the ipcs command to show all memory segments, message queues, and semaphores:

```
$ipcs -a
```

```
------ Shared Memory Segments --------
key          shmid      owner       perms      bytes        nattch
status
0x00000000 6946816    oracle      600        1056768      12          dest
0x00000000 6979585    oracle      600        1056768      12          dest
0x00000000 7012354    vis         600        8589316      10          dest
0x00000000 7045123    oracle      600        1056768      11          dest
0x00000000 7077892    vis         600        1056768      10          dest
0x00000000 7110661    oracle      600        8589316      9           dest

------ Semaphore Arrays --------
key          semid      owner       perms      nsems        status
0x00000000 1081344    oracle      600        1
0x00000000 32769      vis         600
------ Message Queues --------
key          msqid      owner       perms      used-bytes   messages
```

To limit the display of the command, you may use it in conjunction with grep to search for a specific process owner, as shown here:

```
$ipcs -a | grep vis
```

```
0x00000000 7012354    vis         600        8589316      10          dest
0x00000000 7077892    vis         600        1056768      10          dest
0x00000000 32769      vis         600
```

Additional parameters for the ipcs command can be displayed with the following command:

```
$ipcs -help
```

Once the ipcs command has been executed, the memory segment or semaphore can be removed by issuing the ipcrm command. For example, a memory segment can be removed with the following command:

```
ipcrm -m [segment number]
```

In this command, [segment number] is the number of the memory segment for the corresponding process displayed in the ipcs command. Here is an example:

```
$ipcrm -m 7012354
```

A semaphore may be removed with the following command:

```
$ipcrm -s [segment number]
```

In this command, [segment number] is the number of the semaphore for the corresponding the process displayed in the ipcs command.

The following example removes a specific semaphore:

```
$ipcrm -s 32769
```

Finding and Removing Print Jobs

Application users may at times accidentally send large print jobs to the printer. When this occurs, the Applications DBA may be called upon to cancel the print job. This can be achieved by using the lpstat and lprm commands.

To list all of the print jobs for a specific print queue, the following command can be executed:

```
lpstat -p[print queue]
```

In this command, [print_queue] is the name of the UNIX print queue where the job to be cancelled has been sent by the user in the application.

The following example lists all print jobs for a specific print queue:

```
$lpstat -p
```

```
printer lp1 unknown state. enabled since Dec 06 17:31 2005. available
Printer: lp1@sc 'hp4500' (dest TEXT@hp4500)
Queue: 1 printable job
Server: pid 786 active
Unspooler: pid 788 active
Status: sending data file 'dfA785sc' to TEXT@hp4500 at 17:30:39.443
Rank    Owner/ID              Class Job Files                    Size
Time
1       oracle@sc+785           A    785 SYSADMIN.10392083
245212 17:30:39
Active connection from  10.0.0.283 lpd Service
```

To remove a job from the print queue, the lprm command can be executed. Parameters for the lprm command are described in Table 6-12. The syntax for the lprm command is as follows:

```
lprm -P[print queue] [job number]
```

Table 6-12. *Parameters for the* lprm *Command*

Parameter	Description
[print_queue]	The name of the UNIX-defined print queue. This name will match the definition of the printer in the application.
[job_number]	The number of the print job as displayed by the lpstat command for the submitted job that you wish to cancel.

The following example will remove a specific print job:

```
$lprm -P lp1 785
```

Removing Database Sessions

At times it is necessary to remove a session from the database. This can be accomplished with the following steps:

1. Obtain the database session ID and serial number, along with the operating system process ID with a SQL statement. The SQL statement will retrieve the sid and pid for a particular condition:

   ```
   select sid, serial#, pid from v$session where [condition];
   ```

2. Use the sid and serial# to kill the database session:

   ```
   alter system kill session '&sid,&serial#';
   ```

   In this command, &sid and &sid were the values obtained in step 1.

3. Determine, with the ps command, whether the underlying operating system process has terminated. If the process still exists on the server, terminate it with the kill command. Here is an example:

   ```
   ps -ef | grep [process id]
   kill -9 [process id]
   ```

   The [process id] is the pid that was obtained in step 1.

Scheduling Scripts

Scripts can be scheduled to execute at specific times by using the UNIX crontab command, EM 10g Grid Control, or other third-party tools. This section will provide a brief overview of using crontab and EM 10g Grid Control for scheduling jobs.

Using crontab

UNIX jobs can be scheduled by creating entries in the cron table or crontab. Entries in the crontab are then executed by the cron daemon scheduler. This utility is very useful if a tool like EM 10g is not available for your environment. Through crontab, the Applications DBA can run custom scripts on a scheduled basis to perform a variety of tasks. Jobs scheduled through crontab will execute on the server as scheduled, unless the server is down.

Each user has its own crontab to schedule jobs. Entries in the crontab have the layout described in Table 6-13.

Table 6-13. *Layout of Entries in* crontab

Minute	Hour	Day of Month	Month	Day of Week	Command
[0–59]	[0–23]	[1–31]	[1–12 |Jan–Dec]	[0–6 | Sun–Sat]	[command to execute]

To list the crontab entries for a user, issue the following command:

```
$crontab -l
```

```
# At 05:00 every Sunday, stop and restart the Apache server
0 5 * * 0 /oracle/admin/scripts/vis/restart_apache.sh 1>/dev/null ➥
2>/dev/null
. . .
. . .
# At 22:30 every night, execute the backup
30 22 * * * /oracle/admin/scripts/vis/backup.sh 1>/dev/null ➥
2>/dev/null
```

To add entries to or remove them from the crontab, issue the following command:

```
$crontab -e
```

Using crontab -e will open the crontab for editing with the standard text editor. After making the appropriate modifications to the file, simply save it as you would a normal text file.

■**Caution** Only Applications DBAs experienced with UNIX scripting should perform the task of scheduling jobs through `crontab`. Scripts to be run through `crontab` should be carefully tested to ensure they perform the desired operations.

Scheduling and Monitoring Tools

There are many database-monitoring tools available for managing Oracle database systems. These tools all have similar features for monitoring the database.

One feature of EM 10*g* Grid control is the ability to schedule jobs to execute in databases or on the servers. Notification can be sent if the job executes successfully or if there is a failure. Jobs can be created and stored in the job library, and they can be copied and easily modified within the browser framework. The job management and scheduling that is offered by EM 10*g* Grid Control is easy to use and manage via a user-friendly GUI.

In addition to the basic monitoring and scheduling features, EM 10*g* Grid Control has some advantages over other third-party tools. Oracle provides Oracle Applications plug-ins and management packs for EM 10*g* Grid Control that allow you to manage and monitor other components of the E-Business Suite, including the iAS, the server, and Concurrent Manager. Additional information about managing the E-Business Suite with EM 10*g* Grid Control is provided in MetaLink Note 308320.1.

■**Note** The EM Management Packs have additional licensing requirements.

Preventative Maintenance

There are many tasks that need to be performed on a regular basis to maintain the overall health of the Oracle E-Business Suite. Many of these tasks should be scheduled with `crontab`, EM 10*g* Grid Control, or a like utility, or as a concurrent request.

The following preventative maintenance topics will be discussed:

- Gathering statistics
- Recompiling invalid objects
- Rotating log files
- Rebuilding indexes

- Stopping and restarting the Apache Server
- Purging concurrent requests
- Purging workflow history
- Purging and archiving data

Gathering Statistics

Statistics are gathered so that the cost based optimizer (CBO) can determine the best execution plan for queries that are executed. For Oracle Applications, statistics may be gathered with the fnd_stats package or with a few Oracle-standard concurrent requests. Regardless of the method chosen, statistics should be gathered on a regularly scheduled basis. Failure to do so will result in severe performance degradation.

While the frequency with which statistics are gathered is environment specific, it is recommended that you gather stats at least once per week. If an environment experiences frequent data changes throughout the week, this frequency may not be sufficient. Tables with frequent changes may require statistics to be generated after batch processing.

Using fnd_stats

The fnd_stats package is based on the standard Oracle dbms_stats package. It was created to generate statistics for the Oracle E-Business Suite. This package should be executed on the database as the APPS user.

■Caution Do not use the standard dbms_stats package to gather statistics for Oracle Applications; only the fnd_stats package should be used.

These are some of the procedures available for gathering statistics with fnd_stats:

- fnd_stats.gather_schema_statistics: Used to gather statistics for schemas
- fnd_stats.gather_tables_stats: Used to gather table-level statistics
- fnd_stats.gather_column_stats: Used to gather column-level statistics
- fnd_stats.gather_index_stats: Used to gather index statistics

The following example will gather statistics for all schemas:

```
SQL> exec fnd_stats.gather_schema_statistics('ALL')
```

The following example will gather statistics for all objects in the GL schema:

```
SQL> exec fnd_stats.gather_schema_statistics('GL')
```

The following example script can be used to gather statistics:

```
#Script used to generate statistics using fnd_stats
LOGFILE=/tmp/generate_stats_$ORACLE_SID.log
sqlplus -s apps/apps << EOF
  spool $LOGFILE;
  exec fnd_stats.gather_schema_statistics ('ALL)
  spool off;
  exit
EOF
exit 0
```

When running the fnd_stats procedure, it is possible to gather statistics for all or some of the rows in a table. To gather statistics for all rows in a table, the compute option is used with fnd_stats. This is also referred to as *computing statistics*. To analyze a percentage of the rows of the table the estimate option is used with the fnd_stats. This is also referred to as *estimating statistics*.

If the table data is normally distributed, then estimating statistics will provide query optimization. For most objects, either the default of 10 percent, or a value of 30 percent, is sufficient for gathering statistics. When computing or estimating statistics with 50 percent or greater, fnd_stats will analyze all rows of the table. This can be resource intensive for large tables.

The following example will execute fnd_stats for the HR schema with the estimate option set to 30 percent:

```
SQL>exec fnd_stats.gather_schema_statistics('HR', -
> estimate_percent=>30);
```

Oracle provides a script named coe_stats.sql to assist with automating the gathering of statistics. The latest version of this script, and details regarding it, are provided in MetaLink Note 156968.1. Executing the coe_stats.sql script will generate a report called COE_STATS.TXT and a dynamic script called coe_fix_stats.sql. The COE_STATS.TXT report will list all tables that require statistics to be refreshed. The coe_fix_stats.sql script contains the commands required to generate statistics for the tables listed in the report.

Gathering Statistics with Concurrent Requests

Statistics may also be gathered by scheduling standard Oracle concurrent requests. The following is a list of the concurrent requests available to gather statistics:

- Gather schema statistics: Used to gather statistics for schemas
- Gather table statistics: Used to gather table-level statistics
- Gather column statistics: Used to gather column-level statistics
- Analyze all index column statistics: Used to gather index statistics

Reviewing Object-Level Statistics

To determine when an object was last analyzed, the last_analyzed column of the DBA_TABLES or DBA_INDEXES view may be queried. Here is an example:

```
SQL> select table_name, last_analyzed from dba_objects
  2  where owner='GL' and table_name='GL_BALANCES';
```

You may also use the fnd_stats.verify_stats procedure to determine the last-analyzed date for an object. Executing fnd_stats.verify_stats will generate a report. The syntax for the fnd_stats.verify_stats procedure is as follows:

```
fnd_stats.verify_stats ('[schema]', \
'[schema.table_name1, schema.table_name2, . . . ,
schema.table_namen]')
```

Here is an example:

```
SQL> exec fnd_stats.verify_stats('GL', 'GL.GL_BALANCES');
```

Recompiling Invalid Objects

Objects in the database will at times become invalid. While most objects will recompile upon access, sometimes dependencies upon other objects hinder this ability. The following script may be scheduled on a regular basis to assist with recompiling invalid objects in your database:

```
#Script used to recompile invalid objects in the database
LOGFILE=/tmp/recompile_parallel_$ORACLE_SID.log
sqlplus -s sys/change_on_install << EOF
  spool $LOGFILE;
  select count(1) from dba_objects where status='INVALID';
  exec utl_recomp.recomp_parallel(8);
```

```
select count(1) from dba_objects where status='INVALID';
spool off;
exit
EOF
exit 0
```

The following is an example of executing the `recompile_invalids.sh` script:

```
$sh recompile_invalids.sh
```

The following is an example of scheduling the `recompile_invalids.sh` script to execute daily—it is scheduled in the instance owner `crontab` on the database server:

```
# At 06:00 everyday, recompile invalid objects in the database
0 6 * * * /scripts/recompile_invalids.sh 1>/dev/null 2>/dev/null
```

Recompiling invalid objects can also be performed with the `adadmin` utility. To recompile invalids using `adadmin`, first select menu option 3 (Compile/Reload Applications Database Entities), then menu option 1 (Compile APPS schema). Recompiling invalids using `adadmin` is a manual process; however, it allows for a parallel recompile of invalid objects owned by the `APPS` schema.

Rotating Log Files

There are many log files associated with the various components of the E-Business Suite. Over time, these log files will grow in size, and this could cause issues with filesystem free space. It is recommended that log files be rotated on a scheduled basis in order to control potential space issues.

Script for Rotating Log Files

The following sample script will read the contents of a file for a listing of log files and will move each log file listed to `$FILENAME.$DATE`. The script will also remove any log files named `$FILENAME.*` that are older than 30 days.

```
#Script used to rotate and remove log files > 30 days old
#Script name is rotate_logs.sh
LOGFILES=$1
NUM_DAYS_RETAIN=30
DATE=`date +%m%d%y`
#read in list of logfiles
```

```
awk '{print $0}' $LOGFILES | while read FILENAME
do
  # check that file exists.
  if [ -f $FILENAME ]
  then
    # Make sure the entry does not refer to multiple files
    RESULTS=`ls -l $FILENAME | wc -l`
    if [ $RESULTS -gt 1 ]
    then
      exit 1
    fi
    # backup file and remove old copies
    cp $FILENAME $FILENAME.$DATE
    cp /dev/null $FILENAME
    find . -name "$FILENAME.*" -a -mtime +NUM_DAYS_RETAIN -exec rm {}
\;
  fi
done
```

The file read by the script would contain something like this:

```
$cat logfiles.txt
```

```
/u01/oratop/iAS/Apache/Apache/logs/error_log
```

```
/u01/oratop/iAS/Apache/Jserv/logs/jserv.log
```

```
/u01/oratop/8.0.6/network/log/sqlnet.log
```

Here is how you might execute the script file:

```
$sh rotate_logs.sh logfiles.txt
```

The rotate_logs.sh script could be scheduled to execute daily in the instance owner crontab as follows:

```
# At 04:00 everyday, stop and restart the Apache server
0 4 * * * /scripts/restart_apache.sh /scripts/logfiles.txt ➥
1>/dev/null 2>/dev/null
```

Locations of Log Files

There have been many discussions regarding log files in this guide. For quick reference, the locations and descriptions of log files are provided in Table 6-14. Some of these log files are ideal candidates for rotating and subsequent deletion, as discussed in the previous section.

Table 6-14. *Location and Description of Common Log Files*

Log File Location	Description
$APACHE_TOP/Apache/log	Log files for the Apache Server
$APACHE_TOP/Jserv/log	Log files for the JServ
$APACHE_TOP/Jserv/log/jvm	Log files for the JServ
$APPLCSF/$APPLLOG	Log files for concurrent requests
$APPLCSF/$APPLLOG	GSM log file
$COMMON_TOP/admin/log/$CONTEXT_NAME	Log files for patching
$APPL_TOP/admin/$CONTEXT_NAME/log/ MMDDhhmm	AD Config log files
$ORACLE_HOME/appsutil/log/ $CONTEXT_NAME/MMDDhhmm	AD Config log files (database server)
Location defined by database initialization parameter bdump	Database alert[ORACLE_SID].log
Location defined by database initialization parameter udump	SQL-generated trace files
Location defined by listener.ora parameter LOG_DIRECTORY_LISTENER	Database listener log file

Rebuilding Indexes

As data in the database is updated and deleted and new records are inserted, indexes will lose effectiveness. In order to prevent performance issues that may occur due to inefficient indexes, indexes should be rebuilt periodically. As with other preventative maintenance, the frequency with which indexes are rebuilt is environment specific.

Oracle provides a script called bde_rebuild.sql that can be used to validate and rebuild indexes. MetaLink Note 182699.1 contains the latest version of the bde_rebuild.sql script and details regarding its execution.

The bde_rebuild.sql script will generate a report called BDE_REBUILD_REPORT.TXT that contains a report on the indexes. A dynamic SQL script called bde_rebuild_indexes.sql contains the SQL required to rebuild indexes that are consuming more space than the specified threshold.

Depending upon the size of your indexes, the index rebuild may take a long time and use an excessive amount of redo logging. If you are running the instance in archivelog mode, be sure to have adequate free space in your archive log directory.

■**Tip** Indexes can be rebuilt online; however, it is recommended that such maintenance tasks be scheduled during periods of low database activity.

Stopping and Restarting the Apache Server

At times, it is necessary to stop and restart (bounce) the Apache Server. This removes JDBC thin client connections that have not cleanly disconnected from the database, and it also allows application configuration changes, such as personalizations, to take effect. Between the stop and restart of the Apache Sever, it is also recommended that that the Apache cache be removed.

How often you should bounce the Apache Server depends on your environment. The following script can be used to schedule the Apache Server bounce:

```
-- You may need to alter where the script looks for '_pages'
-- depending upon
-- your environment
LOGFILE=/tmp/bounce_apache_$ORACLE_SID.log
$COMMON_TOP/admin/scripts/$CONTEXT_NAME/adapcctl.sh stop > $LOGFILE
if [ -d $COMMON_TOP/_pages ]
then
   rm -r $COMMON_TOP/_pages/* >>$LOGFILE
fi
$COMMON_TOP/admin/scripts/$CONTEXT_NAME/adapcctl.sh start >> $LOGFILE
```

Purging Concurrent Requests

When concurrent requests are scheduled, history is kept in tables in the database. Log and output files are also created on the Concurrent Processing Node. Over time, as more and more requests are scheduled and executed, the associated tables and number of log and output files can become quite large. Oracle provides a standard concurrent request, called Purge Concurrent Request and/or Manager Data, FNDCPPUR, to purge the table history as well as the associated log and output files.

This schedule should be executed daily. The amount of history maintained will be system dependent. If there are any legislative or legal requirements to maintain the history for longer periods of time, the files can be backed up to tape prior to removal. The job can be scheduled to maintain a specified number of days of history. If this job is not scheduled, performance degradation can be experienced with Concurrent Manager processing.

The first time this job is scheduled, it may be necessary to run several iterations with older history settings, in order to prevent errors resulting from excessive undo tablespace usage.

■**Tip** It is recommended that you maintain no more than 30 days of online history for Concurrent Manager processing.

Purging Workflow History

Workflow history is also kept in tables in the database. Based upon the amount of activity in your application, the size of the underlying workflow-related tables can increase dramatically. This increase in size will eventually cause performance degradation.

Oracle has provided a standard concurrent request called Purge Obsolete Workflow Runtime Data, FNDWFPR to purge workflow history. It is recommended that this request be scheduled to execute daily. The job can be scheduled to maintain a specified number of days of history.

Purging and Archiving Data

While it is beyond the scope for this guide to provide details regarding how to purge and archive data contained in the E-Business Suite, it is worth mentioning that a purge and archive strategy should be documented and implemented for your environment. Oracle provides purge routines for many of the primary modules of the application, and these routines may be used to delete data according to the requirements of your organization.

The benefits of controlling data growth include reducing expenses for disk space. More importantly, performance can be vastly improved by reducing the row size of large tables.

Application Instance Clones

Cloning is a method for copying an application instance and database to a
test application instance and database. Clones are often required for development and testing purposes. Details for creating instance clones are
considered beyond the scope of this guide, as methods for cloning vary
according to the application release level and the system architecture.
However, some general information will be provided in this section.

Using Rapid Clone

Oracle's recommended method for cloning is to use the Rapid Clone utility.
Oracle provides the following MetaLink Notes to assist with this process:
230672.1 and 216664.1. Before cloning, be sure to carefully review the entire
contents and additional prerequisite requirements outlined in these
MetaLink notes.

■**Tip** As part of the testing process for a major upgrade, test the cloning process.
Upgrades quite often will modify cloning requirements.

There is functionality built into OAM to assist with cloning. These wizards can be accessed from the Site Map ➤ Maintenance ➤ Cloning menu
options. Two wizards, Simple Clone and Advanced Clone, are available
depending upon your requirements. If these wizards are to be used for
cloning, thoroughly test the steps before attempting a clone from your production system. A portion of the Clone Status screen, which includes links
to the clone wizards, is shown in Figure 6-4.

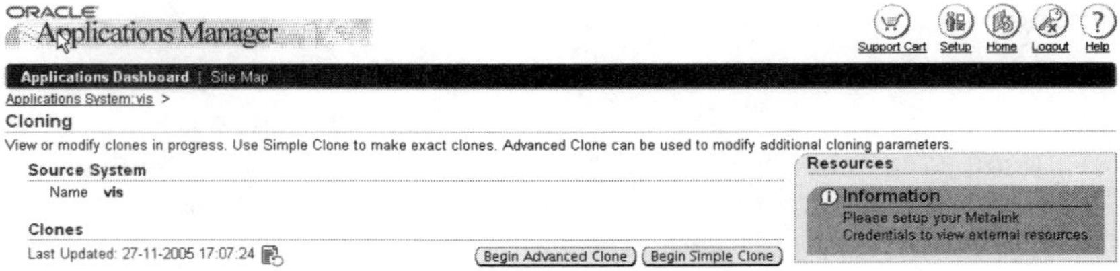

Figure 6-4. *OAM clone wizards*

Tip Sometimes a full application and database clone may not be necessary. If the APPL_TOP has not been modified by applying application patches, it is possible to perform a database-only clone to provide current production data to the test instance.

Cloning Cleanup

There are several post-cloning steps that must be performed. Currently the Rapid Clone utility does not clean up workflow-related tables or profiles other than site-level profiles. Additionally, if printer requirements differ, new printers will need to be defined in the cloned instance. Many of these post-cloning steps may be scripted and called as post-cloning cleanup. The post-cloning steps for this process are described in MetaLink Note 230672.1.

Other post-cloning steps are environment dependent. For example, you may want to add steps to change the APPS password in the target environment, remove the files from the APPLCSF directory in order to save space in the target APPL_TOP filesystem, and end-date accounts to restrict access to the test instance.

Tip Do not end-date the GUEST or SYSADMIN account in the application, as it will render the application unusable until the accounts are un-end-dated.

## CHAPTER 7

Resources

There are a variety of resources available to Applications DBAs that can be utilized to expand your knowledge and provide support for your day-to-day tasks. The resources that will be discussed in this chapter are as follows:

- **Oracle Support**: This section will look at MetaLink, Oracle Support's web site, and cover searching for tips, reviewing product and OS platform certification combinations, and the various aspects of Oracle Service Requests.

- **User communities and conferences**: This section will outline the key user groups and conferences for Oracle Applications DBAs.

- **Online resources**: This section will outline additional online resources.

- **Books and periodicals**: This section will offer tips for finding additional printed materials covering topics of interest for the Oracle Applications DBA.

Working with Oracle Support

Managing the E-Business Suite includes interacting with Oracle Support. The main interface to Oracle Support is its web site, MetaLink, http:// metalink.oracle.com. MetaLink is one of the most important resources for an Applications DBA. The site is Oracle's primary location for information about all Oracle product support, including the E-Business Suite and Oracle Database. On MetaLink, you can search Oracle's Notes, Bulletins, Alerts, Bug Database, and User Forums. MetaLink is also the site for managing Service Requests (SRs) and downloading patches for Oracle products.

A user's ability to use all the features available on MetaLink depends on the privileges that have been granted to his or her account.

MetaLink Search Techniques

The most common use of MetaLink is as a technical repository. Searching MetaLink is the best starting point for finding information on a specific topic, such as an error message or a general question. This section will cover basic searches, advanced searches, and tips for locating information on E-Business Suite, reviewing certification matrices, and downloading patches.

Knowledge Base Searches

The Knowledge Base search feature is immediately available upon connecting to MetaLink. To initiate a search, type a search string in the text box located at the top of the screen. Click the Go button to view the results. Sample output from a search for information about "ORA-600" errors is shown in Figure 7-1.

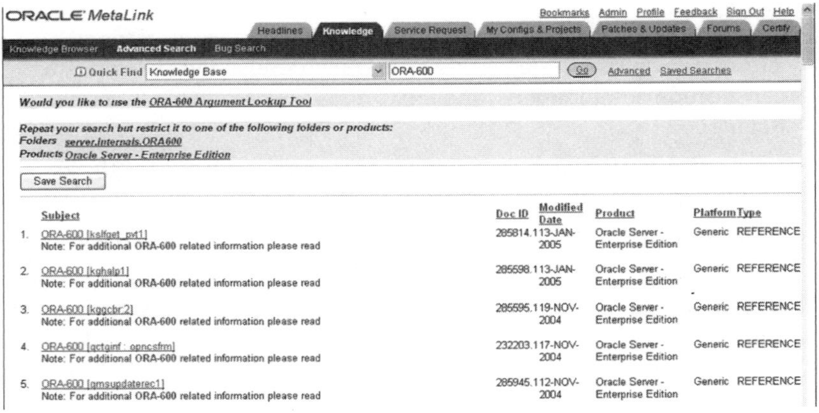

Figure 7-1. *An example of MetaLink's basic search*

Advanced Searches

If the results returned from the Knowledge Base searches are insufficient, or you want to limit the result set, you can click the Advanced Search button to execute a more detailed search. Within the Advanced Search section, you can customize your search to return a more focused result group. For example, if you want to limit your result set to only Oracle-provided Notes, the Technical Forum source can be unselected.

Other options found in the Advanced Search screen (shown in Figure 7-2) include a variety of text fields for refining the search parameters. There are also some fields for changing the weighting values of the search's result set. From this screen, you can also limit the start date for the search, in order to restrict older documents.

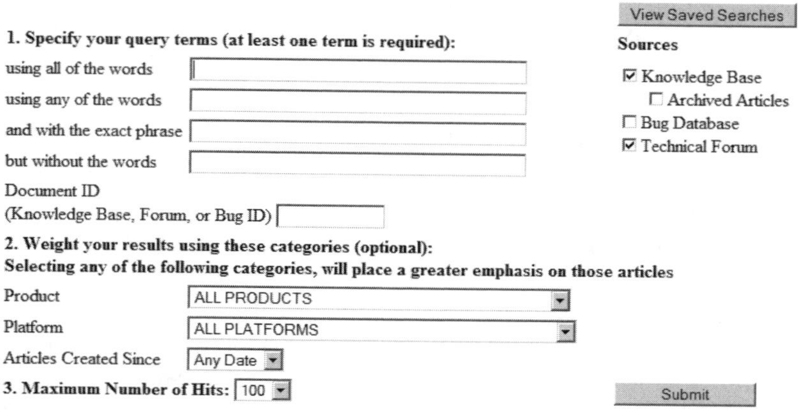

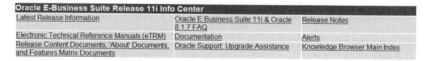

1. Specify your query terms (at least one term is required):

using all of the words

using any of the words

and with the exact phrase

but without the words

Document ID
(Knowledge Base, Forum, or Bug ID)

View Saved Searches

Sources

☑ Knowledge Base
    ☐ Archived Articles
☐ Bug Database
☑ Technical Forum

2. Weight your results using these categories (optional):
Selecting any of the following categories, will place a greater emphasis on those articles

Product   ALL PRODUCTS

Platform   ALL PLATFORMS

Articles Created Since   Any Date

3. Maximum Number of Hits: 100

Submit

Figure 7-2. *Advanced Search capabilities in MetaLink*

E-Business Information

The MetaLink home page includes a link labeled E-Business 11i. Selecting this link takes you to the Oracle E-Business Suite Info Center. This page is an excellent starting point for Applications DBAs to conduct research for information about the E-Business Suite. The links available from this page are shown in Figure 7-3.

Oracle E-Business Suite Release 11i Info Center		
Latest Release Information	Oracle E Business Suite 11i & Oracle 8.1.7 FAQ	Release Notes
Electronic Technical Reference Manuals (eTRM)	Documentation	Alerts
Release Content Documents, 'About' Documents, and Features Matrix Documents	Oracle Support: Upgrade Assistance	Knowledge Browser Main Index

Figure 7-3. *The E-Business Suite information portal on MetaLink*

From this screen, the Applications DBA can obtain information about the latest releases of the applications and the latest relevant documentation. Links for documentation include Release Content and About documents, Release Notes, and all Oracle E-Business Suite documentation and manuals. This page also contains links to the Electronic Technical Reference Manuals (eTRM), which display E-Business Suite database design and dependency information.

Certification Matrix

Information related to product availability and about certification for different platforms and versions can be obtained from the certification matrix.

Selecting the Certify tab on MetaLink will allow you to access this feature. Certification information may be searched by the criteria on the Certify page, as shown in Figure 7-4.

1. View Certifications by Product
2. View Certifications by Platform
3. View Product Availability

Figure 7-4. *Certification and availability options in MetaLink's Certify page*

After selecting the desired search option, you will be able to select the operating system platform and product combination for which you want to view certification information. The matrix returned by the search includes links for Additional Information, Components, Other, and Issues. These links should also be consulted when investigating certified combinations, as they may also contain important information.

■**Tip** Prior to performing any technology stack component upgrade, the certification matrix on MetaLink should be reviewed. Ensure that the versions for the products to be upgraded are certified for your operating system.

Locating and Downloading Patches

MetaLink is the source for downloading patches for the Oracle E-Business Suite components. There are many options when searching patches, as displayed in Figure 7-5.

Patches

Note: Full support customers may submit technical, patch related questions for Oracle products using the MetaLink iTAR functionality. Japanese users may contact support via OiSC or VSA.

- Simple Search
- Advanced Search
- eBusiness Suite Recommended Patch List
- Quick Links to the Latest Patchsets, Mini Packs, and Maintenance Packs
- Your Saved Searches

Figure 7-5. *Patch Search Options in MetaLink*

- **Simple Search**: This option will allow you to find a patch when you have the patch number and specify the platform or language.

- **Advanced Search**: This option will allow you to search based on the criteria displayed in Figure 7-6.

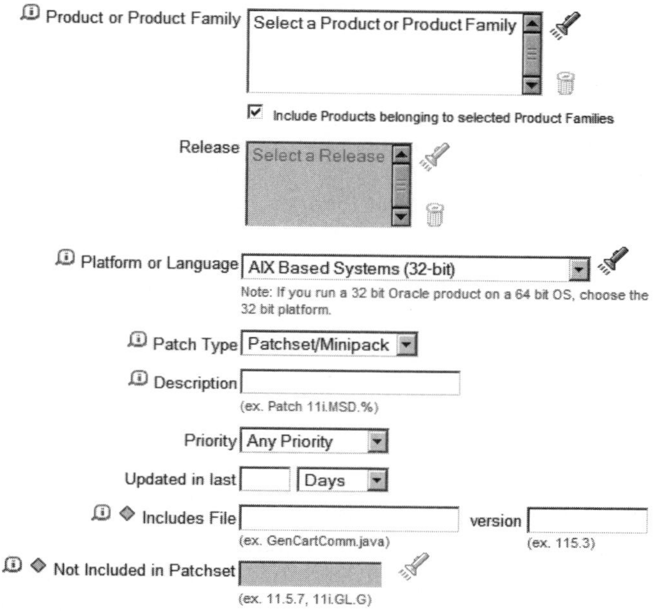

Figure 7-6. *Advanced Search Options in MetaLink*

- **eBusiness Suite Recommended Patches**: This option will allow you to search for E-Business patches by Maintenance Release, Consolidated Update, or Published Date, as well as by the Product Family.

- **Quick Links to the Latest Patchsets, Mini Packs, and Maintenance Packs**: This option will take you to the latest patches available for the E-Business Suite.

- **Your Saved Searches**: This option allows you to access your saved patch searches.

Once a patch has been located, clicking the Download button will download it to your workstation.

■Tip Patches frequently become obsolete or are superseded. Information regarding obsolete or superseded patches is automatically displayed when you search for a patch. When researching which patches you should apply, you should consider replacing obsolete or superseded patches with their new patch replacement.

Oracle Support Service Requests

Part of the management of the E-Business Suite will require you to obtain assistance from Oracle Support. Due to the complexity of the applications, customers are frequently required to initiate Service Requests (SRs). The overall performance and availability of your applications can be improved by effectively managing the SR process. This section will enhance your understanding of the SR process by outlining tips for opening and managing SRs.

■Note Service Requests were previously referred to as Technical Assistance Requests (TARs). Some information on MetaLink may still refer to TARs.

Details for an SR

Prior to opening an SR, gather as much information as possible regarding your environment and the problem being experienced. At a minimum, you should have a one-sentence description of the problem, and any applicable error codes and messages that are generated. Any additional information that you can provide will assist in expediting SR resolution. For example, you should consider running provided diagnostics utilities, generating trace files, or setting debugging levels to capture additional information for Oracle Support. The captured information can be uploaded to the SR when it is opened, or at any time after the SR is created. For ease of transmission, multiple files should be zipped prior to uploading to Oracle Support.

When opening an SR, it is possible to use the My Configs and Projects feature of MetaLink. This feature allows you to define environment-specific information, such as the versions of the various components and any recently applied patches or configuration modifications. By using a tool provided by Oracle, information supplied by My Configs and Projects can be automatically collected or manually added. (For additional information regarding My Configs and Projects refer to MetaLink Note 250434.1.) Other users with the same Customer Support Identifier (CSI) may then use a defined project or configuration when creating a new SR.

Each registered MetaLink user is associated with at least one CSI. The CSI allows Oracle Support to track the customer's support and licensing information. Many organizations have multiple CSI numbers.

Using My Configs and Projects is beneficial, as it eases the process of opening SRs. It prevents the possibility of posting inaccurate information in the SR and eliminates the need to post duplicate information for multiple SRs for the same environment.

SR Severity Level

When an SR is created, it is assigned a severity level. Prior to opening an SR, you should determine the severity level the request should be assigned. This severity level will provide Oracle Support with a notion of the importance of the problem. The severity level of an SR may be modified throughout its life. (An explanation of how to modify the severity level of an SR will be provided later in this section.)

There are four severity levels (SEVs) for SRs:

- **Severity 1**: Complete loss of service for production or mission-critical applications
- **Severity 2**: Partial loss of service
- **Severity 3**: Minor loss of service
- **Severity 4**: No loss of service

When a Severity 1 SR is created, or when an existing SR has its severity level raised to Severity 1, the customer must provide contact information for primary and secondary contacts as well as a management contact. A business justification must also be provided for a Severity 1 SR. As such, Severity 1 SRs should be reserved for true emergencies. Severity 1 SRs require 24 × 7 work from the customer as well as Oracle Support.

Creating an SR

On the MetaLink web site, there is a link for Service Requests. This page will display the option to create a new SR. Upon creation, you will first need to provide the product name and version, platform and version, and database version. You will also be required to enter a CSI number. If your company has multiple CSI numbers, be certain to associate the SR with the appropriate one. In lieu of providing this information every time, you may save a profile with this basic information. SR profiles may be selected upon SR creation.

Subsequent screens will prompt you for a description of the problem as well as related configuration and log files. The SR can be tracked by the number it is assigned upon creation. SRs should be created as soon as it is determined that the issue cannot be resolved without the assistance of Oracle Support. Postponing the creation of an SR will only result in delaying resolution.

Managing an SR

This section will provide some guidance to efficiently working with Oracle Support once an SR has been created.

Searching SRs

If multiple SRs have been logged, it may be difficult to locate a particular SR created by yourself or another user. Finding a specific SR is often necessary if a user has asked for your assistance or if you need to find a problem resolution that is documented in a closed SR.

To search SRs that have been logged, log in to MetaLink and navigate to the SR management section of the site. SRs may be searched and sorted with the following options:

- **Support Identifier**: This will return all SRs for the specified CSI.

- **Products**: This will return all SRs for the selected product. Note that the default search is for ALL PRODUCTS.

- **Severity**: This will return all SRs for the selected severity; the options are the four severity levels.

- **Status**: This will return all SRs for the selected status; the options are open or closed.

- **Last Update**: This will return all SRs for the selected product; the options are yesterday, 2–7 days, 14 days, 30 days, 60 days, 90 days, 120 days, 240 days, and 365 days. The default search is for 90 days.

- **Sort By**: This will sort the SRs by the selected option; the options are Platform, Product, Name, Support Identifier, Last Update, Status, and Severity. The default sort is by Last Update.

After executing the search, the list of SRs displayed on the screen includes the following information:

- SR number
- Severity level for the SR
- Description of the SR
- Last date the SR was updated
- Owner of the SR
- Status of the SR

Updating SRs

The status of the SR will determine whether you need to perform any actions. For example, if the status is set to 1st Callback, the SR has not been updated. If the SR is at a status such as Waiting on Customer, the customer is required to give an update.

Provide timely updates in order to expedite issue resolution. Typical customer requests include providing configuration, trace, or log files, running scripts, applying a patch, or modifying the configuration.

If you are unable to provide updates or implement recommendations for an SR, then you can request that the SR be *soft closed*. A soft closed SR is one that is not actively monitored by Support, but that can be updated by the customer for a specified duration. If the SR is not updated within the time allotted, it will automatically be closed by Support.

Escalating an SR

If you feel that your SR is not receiving appropriate attention, you can update it and request an updated action plan from the analyst. The next level of escalation would be to request that a duty manager contact you in order to discuss the SR.

The fastest way to escalate an SR is to phone in the request. If you update the SR through the MetaLink web site, you may not be contacted until the next business day. Additional details for effectively working with Oracle Support are outlined in MetaLink Note 166650.1

■**Tip** MetaLink will set the status of an SR to Immediate Response Required if the client provides three successive updates.

SRs should only be escalated if the issue is severe enough to warrant such action. Overusing or misusing escalation features does not provide any benefit to the customer. When escalating an SR or changing the severity level, be sure to perform the action early enough for Oracle Support to respond to your needs. Working with Oracle Support, or any other organization's support staff, is a team process. By providing timely and accurate updates, you help ensure that your issues are resolved as quickly as possible.

Escalating an SR does not raise the severity level of the SR. If you need to change the severity level, update the SR with a request to raise the severity level, or phone in a request. Raising the severity level of an SR is necessary if there has been a major status change related to the SR subject, such as a project due date being altered.

SR Codes

SRs are frequently updated with different status codes or bug codes. If development is involved in the Support process, bug codes are provided in the status of the SR.

A description of SR status codes can be found in Table 7-1. A description of the bug codes is in Table 7-2.

Table 7-1. *SR Status Codes*

Code	Description
NEW	New SR
XFR	SR transfer
ASG	Assigned
WIP	Work in progress
RVW	Review
1CB	1st callback
2CB	2nd callback
IRR	Immediate response required
INT	Awaiting internal response
WCP	Waiting for customer to apply patch
CUS	Waiting on customer
SLP	Sleep until customer available
LMS	Left message
SCL	Soft close
HCL	Hard close
DEV	Assigned to development

Table 7-2. *SR Bug Codes*

Code	Description
10	Description phase
11	Code bug
13	Doc bug
14	Bug assigned to solution partner
15	To internal review
16	Support bug screening
30	Additional information requested
31	Could not reproduce
32	Not a bug
33	Suspended, required information not available
35	To filer for review

Code	Description
36	Duplicate bug
37	To filer for review/merge
39	Approved, waiting for codeline to open
40	Waiting for base bug fix
43	Product/platform obsolete
44	Not feasible to fix
45	Vender OS problem
51	Support approved backport
52	Pending approval
53	Backport/patchset request rejected
60	Awaiting promote
66	Awaiting deployment
70	Closed—user error
71	Closed—data import
72	Closed—code error
73	Closed—unknown
74	Closed, verified by QA
80	Development to QA
81	QA to dev or workaround available
83	Closed, product/platform obsolete
84	Closed, not feasible to fix
87	Fix verified
90	Closed, verified by filer
91	Closed, could not reproduce
92	Closed, not a bug
93	Closed, not verified by filer
95	Closed, vendor OS problem
96	Closed, duplicate bug

Requesting Collaborative Support

Issues that are not making sufficient progress towards resolution or that are difficult to communicate in the context of the SR may benefit from using the Oracle Collaborative Support. This feature allows the analyst from Oracle to establish a web conference with you. By doing this, they are able to see your desktop while you reproduce an error.

Collaborative Support is also useful when the analyst has numerous troubleshooting steps that would require a great deal of communication time to work through. The analyst can observe as the steps are performed and provide you with immediate feedback rather than waiting for SR updates.

Phoning Oracle Support

Due to the vast number of features available online, it is rare that Support is contacted by phone. However, in the event that this is required, the number for contacting Oracle Support is 1-800-223-1711. Have your SR number ready when you call.

Closing an SR

Finally, when an SR has been resolved by the client or with the help of the analyst, you can select the Close SR link on the SR update screen. This will remove the SR from the list of active SRs, thereby allowing the analysts to work on other issues. When closing the SR, an optional input text box for entering resolution details will be displayed. It is beneficial for Support to know the steps that resolved the issue.

User Communities and Conferences

There is an extensive user community for Oracle Applications and Oracle Databases. You can use these resources as a source of information and assistance. Sometimes it is valuable to have feedback from people outside of Oracle.

User Groups

There are two major user groups for Oracle Applications and Databases: the Oracle Applications Users Group (OAUG) and the Independent Oracle Users Group (IOUG).

Oracle Applications Users Group

The OAUG was founded in 1990 with the stated mission of representing the interests of Oracle Applications users worldwide in securing the optimum use and ongoing development of the Oracle Applications products. Membership in the OAUG provides the Applications DBA with a wealth of information related to that role. In addition to the existing content found on the OAUG web site, http://www.oaug.org, there are numerous educational opportunities. The web site also contains details regarding membership dues.

The OAUG consists of numerous Special Interest Groups (SIGs) and Geographic User Groups (GEOs). The list of SIGs and GEOs is maintained on the OAUG web site. Review the list of SIGs for groups related to your interests. For Applications DBAs, the Database and Middleware SIGs are good sources of technical Oracle E-Business Suite information. Other SIGs that might be applicable to your interests include product-specific SIGs. Look for GEOs close to your location for opportunities to interact with regional colleagues.

SIGs and GEOs modify their scope frequently, so you should periodically review their availability. It is not a requirement to be a member of the OAUG in order to join a SIG or GEO. You may register as a SIG member on its web site.

Independent Oracle Users Group

The IOUG is a user group dedicated to technical users of Oracle Database. The focus of this user group includes education, networking, and advocacy. Unlike the OAUG, the IOUG is not focused on Oracle Applications. The IOUG contains many excellent services that the Applications DBA can utilize for application technology stack components.

As with the OAUG, there are many regional groups (RUGs) that provide excellent networking opportunities. These RUGs can be found from the main IOUG web site, http://www.ioug.org. In addition to the regional groups and other networking opportunities, the IOUG provides extensive technical reference material within its Technical Repository. Book reviews, monthly tips, and links to online resources are also available from the IOUG web site.

Conferences

Conferences are an excellent source of information for Oracle Applications DBAs. In addition to the sessions, there are numerous keynote addresses that provide insight into the future direction of the products. Of even more value is the opportunity to network with other professionals involved with the E-Business Suite.

Collaborate

The Collaborate conference is an Oracle User Group conference consisting of the OAUG, IOUG, and Quest International Users Group. These groups have combined their yearly conferences to better serve their user communities. The conference has a day devoted to SIG meetings, with the remaining time spent on selected presentations. The combined conference will cover a wide variety of material for Applications DBAs and functional users of the E-Business Suite.

Oracle Open World

The Oracle Open World (OOW) conference is the largest annual Oracle con-ference. Open World includes topics related to Oracle Applications, Oracle middleware, and Oracle Databases, among other subjects.

OOW may be even better known for the numerous keynote sessions provided by the leaders of the technological community. These keynotes include a regular address from Larry Ellison on the future direction of the corporation. The conference also includes a demonstration area where the Applications DBA can see demos of Oracle products and vendor products that can assist in the management of Oracle systems.

Online Resources

This section will cover some of the additional web-based resources available to the Applications DBA. This information can help you expand your skill sets.

Oracle Web Site

Over time, the Applications DBA may become so accustomed to using the MetaLink site that the features available from Oracle's corporate site and the Oracle Technology Network (OTN) section of Oracle's web site are over-looked.

The main corporate site of Oracle Corporation, http://www.oracle.com, provides a wealth of information regarding Oracle products. The material is not only limited to product information, but also includes customer case studies, market data, and corporate data. Additionally, web seminars describing new products or new features of existing products are readily available.

Additional technical information can be obtained by accessing the OTN web site, http://www.oracle.com/technology. Membership to the OTN web site is free. The site is a great source for detailed information about products and features. From this site, users can download products and any required documentation for testing. OTN also provides numerous articles, sample code, and discussion forums, among other resources.

Additional Community Resources

In addition to the well-defined user groups and official Oracle web site, there is the broader Oracle community. A lot of useful information can be found through these resources. Using the Yahoo or Google web search engines, an Applications DBA can find additional information portals.

Many of the web sites that turn up in such searches are companies that post white papers or presentations on their main site. These may include consulting companies interested in providing such information as a means of advertising. Other results may be personal pages of Oracle professionals who are interested in sharing their knowledge with other users. Some consulting companies have regular newsletters that they release on a monthly or quarterly basis, and these newsletters often contain documentation, tips, and other information that you may find useful.

Another unofficial means of sharing information with like-minded professionals is through mailing lists, online forums, or newsgroups. Rather than opening a level 4 SR, an Applications DBA may post a message on a forum seeking responses to a question.

■**Caution** Any information found through forums or personal web page searches should be treated with appropriate caution. Thoroughly test any scripts or commands that come from such sources. You should develop a full understanding of any actions recommended by these sources prior to testing.

Books and Periodicals

Even though there is a great deal of reference material online, there is no replacement for the portability and usability of a good book or magazine. Within the Oracle community, there is a large amount of literature available for Applications DBAs.

Books

An Applications DBA's library should not only include books related to Oracle but also books on other components of the technology stack. A good scripting book can be very useful for DBAs with systems running on the Linux environment.

Here are some books we recommend:

- *Expert Oracle Database Architecture: 9i and 10g Programming Techniques and Solutions* by Thomas Kyte
- *Expert Oracle Database 10g Administration* by Sam Alapati
- *Unix for Oracle DBAs Pocket Reference* by Donald Burleson
- *Cost-Based Oracle Fundamentals* by Jonathan Lewis

- *Oracle PL/SQL Programming* by Steven Feuerstein
- *Oracle Wait Interface: A Practical Guide to Performance Diagnostics & Tuning* by Richmond Shee, Kirtikumar Deshpande, and K. Gopalakrishnan

Periodicals

There are several periodicals the Applications DBA would be wise to subscribe to. These magazines contain regular feature articles that provide insight into the latest trends for Oracle Applications and Oracle Database technology, and they should be regular reading for the Applications DBA. These are some of the common magazines:

- *Oracle Magazine*: A free Oracle publication. Current and archived issues of *Oracle Magazine* can be accessed online. A free subscription may also be requested from this site.
- *Profit*: A free Oracle Applications publication. Current and archived issues of *Profit* can be accessed online. A subscription may also be requested online.

■**Tip** Access the following URL for current and archived issues of *Oracle Magazine* and *Profit* and to subscribe: `http://www.oracle.com/oramag/index.html`.

- *SELECT*: An IOUG publication provided to IOUG members.
- *OAUG Insight*: An OAUG publication provided to OAUG members.

In addition to providing insight into product direction, these periodicals include several articles and regular columns that provide tips and techniques for managing Oracle Applications technology stack components.

Final Thoughts

It is important for the Applications DBA to actively participate in the user community. This is not limited to reading articles and attending conferences and user group meetings, although those activities are strongly encouraged. The usefulness of user communities is determined by the participation of its members.

You should look for opportunities to share your knowledge with colleagues and peers. Everyone has unique experiences that can benefit other professionals. Look for areas where you can contribute to this community. Write articles for the periodicals that you read on a regular basis. Develop presentations for conferences or for user group meetings you attend. Contribute to technical forums and newsgroups when possible. Volunteer your time with user groups such as OAUG and IOUG. These organizations will benefit greatly from your input—both groups need assistance from experienced and dedicated professionals like you.

Index

Find it faster at http://superindex.apress.com/

Find it faster at http://superindex.apress.com/

Find it faster at http://superindex.apress.com/

Find it faster at http://superindex.apress.com/

Find it faster at http://superindex.apress.com/

Find it faster at http://superindex.apress.com/

Find it faster at http://superindex.apress.com/

Find it faster at http://superindex.apress.com/

Find it faster at http://superindex.apress.com/

Find it faster at http://superindex.apress.com/

Find it faster at http://superindex.apress.com/

Find it faster at http://superindex.apress.com/

■X

■Z

You Need the Companion eBook

Your purchase of this book entitles you to its companion eBook for only $10.

We believe this Apress title will prove so indispensable that you'll want to carry it with you everywhere, which is why we are offering the companion eBook for $10 to customers who purchase this book now. Convenient and fully searchable, the eBook version of any content-rich, page-heavy Apress book makes a valuable addition to your programming library. You can easily find, copy, and apply code, and then perform examples by quickly toggling between instructions and the application. Even simultaneously tackling a donut, diet soda, and complex code becomes simplified with hands-free eBooks!

Once you purchase this book, getting the $10 companion eBook is simple:

❶ Visit **www.apress.com/promo/tendollars/**.

❷ Complete a basic registration form to receive a randomly generated question about this title.

❸ Answer the question correctly in 60 seconds and you will receive a promotional code to redeem for the $10 eBook.

2560 Ninth Street • Suite 219 • Berkeley, CA 94710

Apress eBookshop   ASP Today   Apress THE EXPERT'S VOICE™

All Apress eBooks subject to copyright protection. No part may be reproduced or transmitted in any form or by any means, electronic or mechanical, including photocopying, recording, or by any information storage or retrieval system, without the prior written permission of the copyright owner and the publisher. The purchaser may print the work in full or in part for their own non-commercial use. The purchaser may place the eBook title on any of their personal computers for their own personal reading and reference.

Offer valid through 10/06.

⚡ FIND IT FAST with the ⚡
Apress *SuperIndex*™

Quickly Find Out What the Experts Know

Leading by innovation, Apress now offers you its *SuperIndex*™, a turbocharged companion to the fine index in this book. The Apress *SuperIndex*™ is a keyword and phrase-enabled search tool that lets you search through the entire Apress library. Powered by dtSearch™, it delivers results instantly.

Instead of paging through a book or a PDF, you can electronically access the topic of your choice from a vast array of Apress titles. The Apress *SuperIndex*™ is the perfect tool to find critical snippets of code or an obscure reference. The Apress *SuperIndex*™ enables all users to harness essential information and data from the best minds in technology.

No registration is required, and the Apress *SuperIndex*™ is free to use.

❶ Thorough and comprehensive searches of over 300 titles

❷ No registration required

❸ Instantaneous results

❹ A single destination to find what you need

❺ Engineered for speed and accuracy

❻ Will spare your time, application, and anxiety level

Search now: *http://superindex.apress.com*